Co-Occurring Disorders and Prisoner Reentry

Co-Occurring Disorders and Prisoner Reentry

By

Paul E. Tracy and Danielle Marie Carkin

Cambridge Scholars Publishing

Co-Occurring Disorders and Prisoner Reentry

By Paul E. Tracy and Danielle Marie Carkin

This book first published 2019

Cambridge Scholars Publishing

Lady Stephenson Library, Newcastle upon Tyne, NE6 2PA, UK

British Library Cataloguing in Publication Data
A catalogue record for this book is available from the British Library

ISBN (10): 1-5275-3903-2
ISBN (13): 978-1-5275-3903-7

TABLE OF CONTENTS

List of Tables

List of Figures

CHAPTER ONE

INTRODUCTION

Beginning in 1999, public policy concern and research interest in the United States started to focus on the issue of offender reentry back into society. Petersilia was among the first to call attention to the issue of prisoner reentry when she noted that there had been virtually no systematic, comprehensive attention being paid by policy makers to address the problems offenders must confront after they are released from custody (1999, 2001). While it is true that Petersilia's observation pertained mostly to the many thousands of offenders who were being released on parole, the issue becomes even more manifold when one considers that many jurisdictions had abolished parole in favor of determinate sentences, and these offenders are released without any community supervision whatsoever. Jeremy Travis, the Director of the National Institute of Justice, raised this point specifically when he noted that concerns about offender reentry came at a time when traditional mechanisms for managing reentry had been significantly weakened because 14 states had abolished discretionary parole and the parole boards that had historically overseen the processes of reentry (2000). Indeed, Ditton and Wilson (1999) indicated that approximately 20 percent of state prisoners leave prison with no post-release supervision. Even Janet Reno, the Attorney General at the time referred to reentry as "one of the most present problems we face as a nation, the reentry of offenders from prison back to the communities where the problem started in the first place" (2000).

Trends

It is surprising that serious concern over prisoner reentry did not arise and take hold until 1999. The seeds of the reentry problem were established long before 1999, and available data clearly indicated a reentry problem that likely would not only continue, but also, would increase significantly. One of the significant factors behind the reentry problem was the American "baby boom" phenomenon (Bouvier, 1980). The so-called baby boom began in 1945 and lasted until 1964. More babies were born in 1946 than ever before–3.4 million, 20 percent more than in 1945. In 1947, another 3.8 million babies were born; 3.9 million were born in 1952; and more than 4 million were born every year from 1954 until 1964, when the boom finally tapered off. By then, there were 76.4 million "baby boomers" in the United States. They made up almost 40 percent of the nation's population. Figure1-1 depicts the baby boom phenomenon (Bureau of Census). It also depicts what is referred to as the "baby boom echo." Because baby boomers delayed having children well beyond the ages that their parents had children, another upsurge in births occurred in 1977 and continued with annual increases in the number of births until 1990.

Figure 1-1. Number of Births: 1940-1994

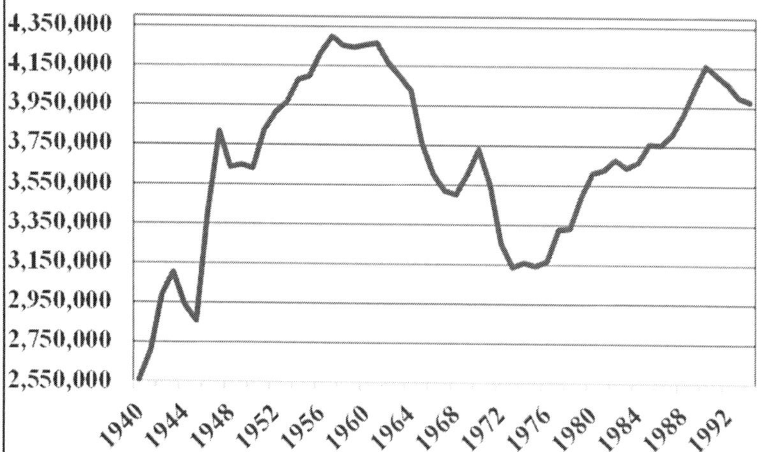

The relationship between age and crime is a well-established topic in criminology. We know that the prevalence of crime starts increasing at around age 15, continues to rise until the mid-20s, and then declines. We also know that crime rates began increasing in 1960 and increased every year until 1980. Is it a coincidence that 1960 is the year at which point the first of the baby boomer cohorts, born in 1945, reached the age of 15? A few researchers investigated the relationship between the baby boom and rise in crime rates in the early 1960s. Sagi and Wellford (1968), reported to the President's Commission on Law Enforcement and the Administration of Justice that shifts in the age composition of the population were a likely explanation. Specifically, Sagi and Wellford (1968) explored the contribution that the post-World War II baby boom generation was making on the crime wave of the 1960s. They reported two major findings. First, during the early 1960s, individuals born in the early years of the baby boom hit peak criminal offending ages (i.e., their late teens and early 20s) and the population increase in these young ages between 1958 (the low point of national crime rates in the late 1950s) and 1964 (the most recent year's data available at the time of the Sagi and Wellford study) accounted for 24 percent of the increase in FBI Index (or UCR Part I) offenses. Second, Sagi and Wellford further demonstrated that the baby boom effects on population and place of residence accounted for 46 percent of the increase in crime rates between 1958 and 1964. Wellford (1973) followed up the previous study and extended the time series to include annual index crime rates through 1969. He found that the rate of violent crimes rose more than that of property crimes among youth during this period. He also reported other disturbing results showing that, with one exception, each cohort born during the baby boom was exhibiting crime rates higher than the one before.

The effect of baby boomers on crime was further explored through the 1970s and 1980s. For example, Greenberg (1985) concluded that among the baby boom cohorts there were high crime-prone cohorts of offenders who likely will not exhibit deceasing crime propensities throughout their life course. Cohen and Land (1987) and Steffensmeier and Harer (1987) reexamined the impact of age composition on crime trends.

Cohen and Land (1987) conducted an analysis of crime trends in the United States through the mid-1980s based on a time-series regression analysis for a somewhat longer post-World War II period, 1946 through 1984, to determine the extent to which changes in the age structure influenced the crime trends. They focused specifically on homicide and motor vehicle theft rates and controlled for other social forces affecting crime rates: trends in business cycles as well as in criminal opportunity and the rate of imprisonment. They first identified the peak ages of offending for homicide and motor vehicle theft, 15 to 29 and 15 to 24, respectively. Using graphical analyses, Cohen and Land demonstrated that the homicide and motor vehicle trends mirrored the trends in age structure for these two youth groups.

Steffensmeier and Harer (1987) used age-specific estimates of the U.S. population produced by the Bureau of the Census through the end of the 20th century to forecast reductions in the nation's crime rate from 1980 to 2000. The forecasts assumed that age-specific offending rates would remain constant into the future and thus were based solely on changes in age composition. Specifically, they noted that the proportion of young people (ages 15-24), those at high risk for property crime, was estimated to decline sharply into the early 1990s and the proportion of youth and young adults (ages 15-35), those at high risk for person crime, was expected to decline steadily. They found that the age composition accounted for approximately 30 to 70 percent of declines in property and robbery crime rates, since the baby boomers had aged past the property crime-prone ages of adolescence and the early twenties. However, violent crimes had not experienced such a large decline as the baby boomers had not quite reached the ages where the violent criminal offending tends to drop—that is, the late 20s and early 30s (1987).

These studies illustrated that the baby boom phenomenon did have an effect on increased crime rates. Consequently, one can expect there to be similar effects on incarceration rates, size of the prison population, and the volume of inmates being released back into society. These data are depicted in Figures 1-2, 1-3, and 1-4 (Bureau of Justice Statistics: National Prisoner Statistics Program, 1978-2016). The data depicted in the charts indicate a clear trend which frames the reentry issue over time. Figure 1-2 shows the imprisonment rate (per 100,000 population) from 1978 to 2016. The rate at which criminals were imprisoned started at 131 per 100,000 in 1978 and rose each and every year, reaching its peak of 506 per 100,000 in 2008. This represents 31 consecutive years of increased use of prison as a form of punishment. From 2009 to 2016 the imprisonment rate declined to a low of 450 per 100,000 in 2016, a rate which is still over 3.5 times higher than in 1978. Figure 1-3 shows the effect on the size of the prison population of the annual increases in the imprisonment rate. In 1978, the prison population was 307,276 inmates. The prison population increased unabated from 1978 to 2010 at which point there were 1,613,083 inmates in prison. This constitutes a 425 percent increase in the prison population. The prison population declined slightly between 2011 and 2016 and reached a low of 1,505,396 in 2016.

The combined effects of rising crime rates and increased imprisonment lead to a dramatic rise in the prison population. The effect on inmate reentry would start to become clear. The concerns raised by Petersilia and Travis take on even greater significance when recent reentry data are examined. The sheer size of the reentry population warrants increased attention. In 2010, 708,677 inmates were released back to their communities (Guerino, Harrison, and Sabol, 2010), and in 2011, 688,384 offenders, approximately 1,885 individuals per day, were released from state or federal custody (Carson and Sobel, 2012). We can be even more definitive concerning the inmate release data. Figure 1-4 indicates that

142,665 inmates were released back into society in 1978 (about 390 inmates per day). From 1978 to 2008 the number of inmates released from state and federal prisons increased annually and reached a peak of 735,651 inmates released which is a 415 percent increase in the reentry population. According to Hughes and Wilson (2002), at least 95 percent of state inmates will ultimately be released. When we include the approximately nine million offenders released from jails annually (Beck, 2006), we realize that offender reentry actually involves orders of magnitude well beyond state and federal prison releases. Given the magnitude of the reentry issue, policymakers, and the general public alike, now expect corrections to "do a better job" by developing evidenced-based practices and programs to facilitate reentry and prevent recidivism. The task will be daunting as evidenced by studies on recidivism.

Figure 1-2. Annual Imprisonment Rate: 1978-2016

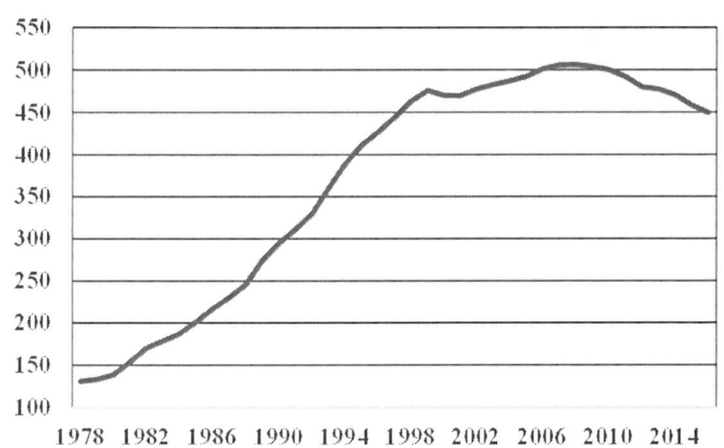

Figure 1-3. Annual Prison Population: 1978-2016

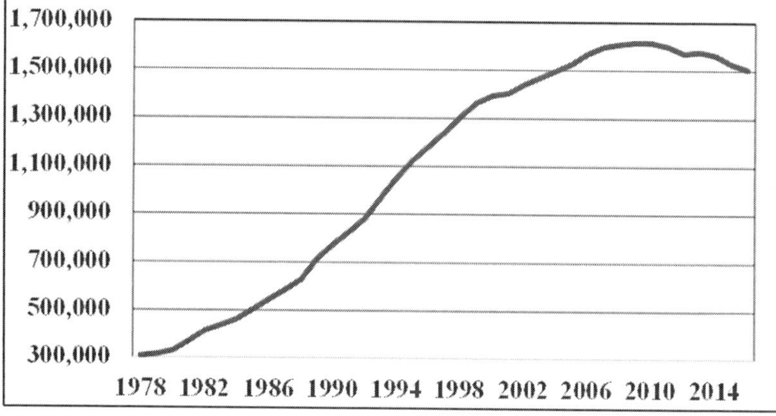

Recidivism

Whatever the original criminogenic factors surrounding the offender's criminal history may have been, community reentry can exacerbate these factors. For example, offenders enter prison with limited marketable work experience, low levels of educational or vocational skills, and many health-related issues, ranging from mental health needs to substance abuse histories and high rates of communicable diseases. Upon release from prison, these challenges persist and affect neighborhoods, families, and society at large (Urban Institute, 2006). The revolving door of prison, release, recidivism, then back to prison is increasingly concentrated in communities that are often already deprived of resources and are not equipped to meet the challenges the reentry population presents (Vigne and Kachnowski, 2003).

Research generally indicates that two-thirds of released prisoners are rearrested within three years of release (Durose, Cooper, and Syder, 2014; Langan and Levin, 2002) and approximately 76 percent will recidivate within five years (Langan and Levin, 2002). Although instructive, there are a few problems with this kind of recidivism data.

First, the samples are usually small and not representative of all inmates being released from prison. So whatever recidivism is found, may be just a function of the kind of cases used.

Figure 1-4. Annual Prison Releases: 1978-2016

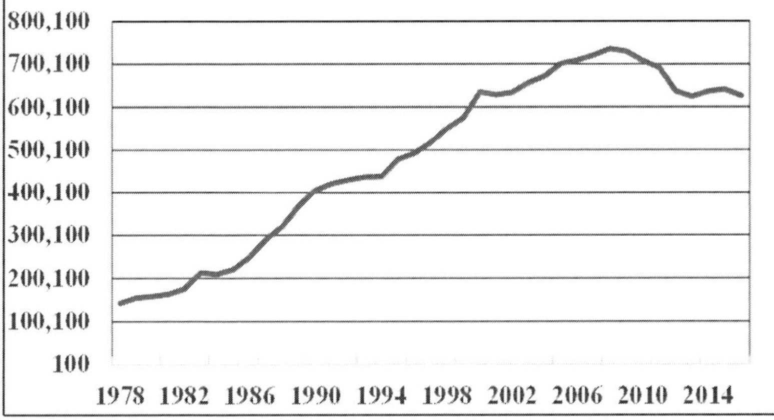

Second, another problem is that the follow-up period is censored and false negatives are entirely possible. That is, with a short follow-up period like one, two or three years, a released prisoner would be classified as a non-recidivist. But, if the clock was allowed to run longer, then more reliable estimates of recidivism would be possible.

Third, although many of these recidivism studies do indicate the time-specific prevalence of recidivism, they fail to indicate the incidence of recidivism across the follow-up period. Thus, we know how many recidivists there are, but not how frequently they are rearrested.

Fortunately, there is a very recent study from the Bureau of Justice Statistics (BJS) which eliminates all these problems and provides definitive data on post release recidivism. The BJS study by Alper and Durose (2018) examined the post-release offending patterns of former prisoners and their involvement in criminal activity both within and outside of the state where they were imprisoned. They employed a very rigorous research design with sophisticated sampling to study 67,966 prisoners who were randomly sampled to represent the 401,288 state prisoners released in 2005 in 30 states. The sample is representative of the 30 states, both individually and collectively. In 2005, these 30 states were responsible for 77 percent of all persons released from state prisons nationwide. The Alper and Durose findings are highly pertinent to the present investigation because they provide longitudinal data on post-release recidivism across all the major demographic characteristics of released prisoners and a very long, nine-year follow-up period. We provide below tables that were extracted from their report.

Table 1-1 provides data (adapted from Alper and Durose, 2018, Table 2) on the percentage of released inmates who recidivated across the nine-year period. The findings are worthy of serious consideration.

First, by the end of the nine years, 83.4 percent of the cases had recidivated at least once. Thus, a prison sentence to punish these criminals and exercise specific deterrence had failed to deter future criminality for 8.3 out of every 10 inmates.

Second, Table 1-1 also provides a year-by-year accounting of the recidivism. These results point to the serious problem surrounding community reentry. That is, 43.9 percent of the sample had been rearrested during the first year of release from prison. In year two, another 17.8 percent had been rearrested which brought the cumulative recidivism total to 60.1 percent. Thus, six out of 10 of the cases had become criminals once again by the end of the second year. This figure rises to 68.4 percent by the end of year three.

Table 1-2 (adapted from Alper and Durose, 2018, Table 3) provides nine-year recidivism data across the major demographic characteristics. Usually in criminological research these data, whether it be the prevalence or incidence of crime, or even the severity, vary considerably across these factors. The researcher must consider the differential criminogenic influences underlying the different factors. Simply, research shows very different crime patters for males v. females, across younger age groups v. older, and across race/ethnicity categories. This time, however, the results shown in Table 1-2 are remarkably consistent. Females only trail males by less than 8 percent. Similarly, across race/ethnicity categories, the highest recidivism percent for African Americans (86.9%) is only greater than the lowest score for Asians, Native Hawaiians, and other Pacific Islanders (79.4%) by 7.5 percent. Usually, the age categories show very disparate differences because crime varies strongly by age. But Table 1-2 indicates that the most crime prone age group of age 24 or younger, only differs by 3 to 5 percent for all other ages except for the oldest category of age 40 or older for which the difference is 13.6 percent. Clearly, the recidivism data across these demographic factors strongly indicate that all released prisoners, regardless of sex, age, or race/ethnicity, exhibit substantial and consistent recidivism over time.

Table 1-3 (adapted from Alper and Durose, 2018, Table 4) provides findings concerning the incidence or extent of post-release recidivism across a nine-year period following release back into the community. Overall, these criminals committed a total of 1,994,000 offenses during the nine years. Further, although over 40 percent were committed in the first three years after release, 31 percent were committed in years four through six, while 28.6 percent were committed in years seven through nine. Thus, sixty percent of these recidivist crimes occurred across a lengthy time span, thus indicating that prior punishment was a minor deterrent, and that reentry was an abysmal failure.

Taken together, the results of the BJS study are instructive. First, 830 out of every 1,000 inmates released back into the community were rearrested. Second, the substantial percentage of recidivism is evident across both sexes and across all age groups and race/ethnicity categories. Last, the criminality of these recidivists was extensive as 1,994,000 arrests were recorded across the nine-year follow-up period.

Table 1-1. Cumulative Percent of Recidivism

Year After		Cumulative Percent	
Release	**Total**	**Arrested**	**Not Arrested**
1	100	43.9	56.1
2	100	60.1	39.9
3	100	68.4	31.6
4	100	73.5	26.5
5	100	77.0	23.0
6	100	79.4	20.6
7	100	81.1	18.9
8	100	82.4	17.6
9	100	83.4	16.6

Source: Alper and Durose, 2018, Table 2

Table 1-2. Recidivism Percent across Nine-Year Follow-Up Period

Characteristic	Within 9 years	Specific Year of Recidivism								
		Year 1	Year 2	Year 3	Year 4	Year 5	Year 6	Year 7	Year 8	Year 9
All released prisoners	83.4%	43.9%	16.2%	8.3%	5.1%	3.5%	2.3%	1.7%	1.3%	1.0%
Sex										
Male	84.2%	44.9%	16.3%	8.3%	5.1%	3.4%	2.3%	1.7%	1.3%	0.9%
Female	76.8	35.1	15.7	8.5	5.5	4.2	2.5	2.2	1.7	1.4
Age at release										
24 or younger	90.1%	51.8%	17.0%	7.7%	4.8%	3.4%	2.0%	1.7%	1.0%	0.7%
25–39	85.3	44.9	16.7	8.6	5.2	3.6	2.3	1.7	1.4	0.9
25–29	87	45.9	16.8	8.8	5.5	3.8	2.5	1.5	1.3	0.9
30–34	84.3	43.9	16.5	8.2	5.3	3.5	2.3	1.9	1.7	1
35–39	84.3	44.6	16.8	8.7	4.9	3.4	2.2	1.7	1.2	0.9
40 or older	76.5	37.8	15.1	8.1	5.1	3.5	2.5	1.9	1.4	1.2
Race/Ethnicity										
White	80.9%	40.2%	15.8%	8.4%	5.2%	3.8%	2.6%	2.2%	1.5%	1.2%
Black/African American	86.9	46	17.4	8.6	5.5	3.4	2.3	1.6	1.2	0.9
Hispanic/Latino	81.3	47.3	14.3	7.2	4.2	3.1	2.2	0.9	1.3	0.7
Other	82.4	44.1	16.4	8.8	4.5	3	1.3	2.1	1.3	1.1
American Indian Alaska Native	85	43.5	16.3	9.5	4.8	3.6	1.6	2.7	1.6	1.4
Asian, Hawaiian, Other Pacific Islander	79.4	45	16	8.3	4	1.3	1.3	1.3	1.2	1

Source: Alper and Durose, 2018, Table 3

Table 1-3. Number and Percent of Recidivism Arrests

Year After Release	Number of Arrests	Percent of Arrests	Cumulative Number	Cumulative Percent
All Years	1,994,000	100%		
1 to 3	804,000	40.3%		
1	306,000	15.4	306,000	15.4
2	260,000	13	567,000	28.4
3	238,000	11.9	804,000	40.3
4 to 6	620,000	31.1%		
4	219,000	11	1,024,000	51.3
5	210,000	10.6	1,234,000	61.9
6	190,000	9.6	1,425,000	71.4
7 to 9	570,000	28.6%		
7	196,000	9.8	1,620,000	81.2
8	194,000	9.7	1,814,000	91
9	180,000	9	1,994,000	100

Source: Alper and Durose, 2018, Table 4

Second Chance Act

The United States Congress took notice of the reentry recidivism problem (as it was documented at the time) and on 9 April 2008 passed H.R. 1593 "The Second Chance Act of 2007: Community Safety Through Recidivism Prevention," also known as Pub. L. 110-199. The *Second Chance Act* was a comprehensive effort to identify and remediate the issues preventing the successful reentry of prisoners back into society. The purposes of the Act were as follows:

- To break the cycle of criminal recidivism, increase public safety, and help states, local units of government, and Indian Tribes, better address the growing population of criminal offenders who return to their communities and commit new crimes;

- To rebuild ties between offenders and their families, while the offenders are incarcerated and after reentry into the community, to promote stable families and communities;

- To encourage the development and support of, and to expand the availability of, evidence-based programs that enhance public safety and reduce recidivism, such as substance abuse treatment, alternatives to incarceration, and comprehensive reentry services;

- To protect the public and promote law-abiding conduct by providing necessary services to offenders, while the offenders are incarcerated and after reentry into the community, in a manner that does not confer luxuries or privileges upon such offenders;

- To assist offenders reentering the community from incarceration to establish a self-sustaining and law-abiding life by providing sufficient transitional services for as short of a period as practicable, not to exceed one year, unless a longer period is specifically determined to be necessary by a medical or other appropriate treatment professional; and

- To provide offenders in prisons, jails or juvenile facilities with educational, literacy, vocational, and job placement services to facilitate reentry into the community (H.R. 1593, p.2).

The Second Chance Act also identified specific programs which might foster and facilitate successful reentry that could be funded under the act, such as the following:

- Providing offenders in prisons, jails, or juvenile facilities with educational, literacy, vocational, and job placement services to facilitate reentry into the community;

- Providing substance abuse treatment and services (including providing a full continuum of substance abuse treatment services that encompasses outpatient and comprehensive residential services and recovery);

- Providing coordinated supervision and comprehensive services for offenders upon release from prison, jail, or a juvenile facility, including housing and mental and physical health care to facilitate reentry into the community, and which, to the extent applicable, are provided by community-based entities (including coordinated reentry veteran-specific services for eligible veterans);

- Providing programs that encourage offenders to develop safe, healthy, and responsible family, and parent-child relationships; and involve the entire family unit in comprehensive reentry services;

- Encouraging the involvement of prison, jail, or juvenile facility mentors in the reentry process and enabling those mentors to remain in contact with offenders while in custody and after reentry into the community;

- Providing victim-appropriate services, encouraging the timely and complete payment of restitution and fines by offenders to victims, and providing services such as security and counseling to victims upon release of offenders;

- Protecting communities against dangerous offenders by using validated assessment tools to assess the risk factors of inmates and developing or adopting procedures to ensure that dangerous felons are not released from prison prematurely (H.R. 1593, p.5).

The responsibility for the administration of the *Second Chance Act* lies with the Bureau of Justice Assistance (BJA), Office of Justice Programs, U.S. Department of Justice. BJA began awarding grants for demonstration projects in 2009, the first federal fiscal year after the act was passed. Table 1-4 displays BJA's grant awards from 2009 through 2017. BJA awarded 150 grants to state, local, and tribal units of government, the total funds awarded amounted to $90,554,503. This level of funding is evidence that prisoner reentry is a significant policy issue and BJA is making funds available under the *Second Chance Act* to impact the problem.

In this study, we are focusing on a particular aspect of the prisoner reentry problem. We are concerned with the co-occurrence or co-morbidity of two risk factors: (1) substance abuse disorders; and (2) mental health disorders. Table 1.5 indicates that BJA has made a concerted effort to fund programs which address the combination of the two risk factors which alone pose serious risks of recidivism, and when they occur together, pose a very high likelihood of post release recidivism. BJA awarded 100 grants and a total of $57,501,975 to address reentry for offenders with co-occurring disorders (COD). This book is an outgrowth of a partnership between the School of Criminology and Justice Studies, University of Massachusetts Lowell, and the Essex County, Massachusetts, Sheriff's Department. Our role was to conduct an evaluation using an experimental design of Essex County's program for Adult Offenders with Co-occurring Disorders through funding from the Bureau of Justice Assistance's *Second Chance Act Reentry Program for Adult Offenders with Co-Occurring Substance Abuse and Mental Health Disorders* (BJA grant #: 2014-RW-BX-0001).

Table 1-4. Second Chance Act Grants: 2009-2017

Year	Number of Awards	BJA State/Local	BJA Tribal	Total
2009	15	$7,732,726		$7,732,726
2010	52	$26,862,343	$462,200	$27,324,543
2011	23	$12,139,765		$12,139,765
2012	11	$5,861,603		$5,861,603
2013	15	$8,628,011		$8,628,011
2014	8	$5,097,359	$694,560	$5,791,919
2015	10	$7,091,609	$682,549	$7,774,158
2016	6	$4,997,302	$997,179	$5,994,481
2017	10	$8,307,297	$1,000,000	$9,307,297
Total	150	$ 86,718,015	$ 3,836,488	**$ 90,554,503**

https://csgjusticecenter.org/nrrc/second-chance-act-innovations-in-reentry-initiative/

Table 1-5. Second Chance Act COD Grants: 2010-2017

Year	Number of Awards	BJA State/Local	BJA Tribal	OJJDP State & Local	Total
2010	**22**	$9,291,018	$407,114	$2,007,723	$11,705,855
2011	**17**	$8,980,972			$8,980,972
2012	**9**	$5,320,710			$5,320,710
2013	**17**	$7,023,158		$2,977,252	$10,000,410
2014	**12**	$7,052,909			$7,052,909
2015	**10**	$5,389,258	$650,000		$6,039,258
2016	**5**	$2,587,645	$650,000		$3,237,645
2017	**8**	$4,514,216	$650,000		$5,164,216
Total	**100**	$50,159,886	$2,357,114	$4,984,975	**$57,501,975**

https://csgjusticecenter.org/nrrc/second-chance-act-co-occurring-disorder-treatment-grant-program/

CHAPTER TWO

REENTRY RISK FACTORS

In addition to the usual deficits in areas like education, employment, vocational skills, etc., areas which represent significant criminogenic factors affecting recidivism, successful prisoner reentry is further compromised by the fact that significant proportions of offenders have substance abuse histories, mental health issues, and most importantly, co-occurring disorders. There is evidence, which continues to grow, that these risk factors affect sizable proportions of returning offenders. Below we review the evidence concerning the prevalence of these three risk factors among justice-involved persons. In order to put the criminal justice venue in proper perspective, we begin each section by reviewing the prevalence of the risk factor among the general population. This provides a baseline with which to examine the criminal justice context.

Substance Abuse

General Population

Table 2-1 provides national data concerning behavioral health trends in the United States (from the 2014 National Survey on Drug Use and Health from the Center for Behavioral Health Statistics and Quality, the Substance Abuse and Mental Health Services Administration (SAMHSA, 2015). These data are the most recent and best source of information concerning national level estimates of substance abuse disorders. The substance use disorder questions used in the survey to classify people as having a substance use disorder in the past 12 months are based on criteria specified in the Diagnostic and Statistical Manual of Mental Disorders (American Psychological Association, 2000). A substance abuse disorder occurs when the recurrent use of alcohol or other drugs (or both) causes clinically significant impairment, including health problems, disability, and failure to meet major responsibilities at work, school, or home (SAMHSA, 2015: 22).

Table 2-1 indicates that among persons 12 years old and older, 21.5 million people, or 8.1 percent, were classified as having a substance use disorder (SUD). The results further showed that 17 million people (6.4%) had an alcohol use disorder, while 7.1 million people (2.6%) had an illicit drug use disorder.

The last column in Table 2-1 provides the percentages using the SUD sub-population as the base. Among those with a substance use disorder, 79 percent had an alcohol use disorder and 32.9 percent had an illicit drug use disorder. Thus, alcohol contributes more than drug use to the substance disorder phenomenon.

It must be noted that the national estimates of SUDS in Table 2-1 (8.1%, 6.4%, and 2.6%) are artificially lower than they probably should be. That is, the data include persons under age 18 in the calculations. It is a certainty that children from 12 to 17 years old do not have anywhere near the prevalence of SUDs as do adults. Consequently, children do not contribute as much to the numerator as do adults. Yet, the 12-18 age group disproportionately contributes to the denominator. The estimated percentages would be higher if only adults were counted. This is a prime example of how important data are not reported in a form that are as usable as they might otherwise be to researchers and to policy makers.

Table 2-1. Substance Use Disorders Age 12 and Over: 2014

	Number in Millions	Percent of Population	Percent of SUD Pop.
Substance Use Disorders	21.5	8.1	100
Alcohol Use Disorder	17	6.4	79
Illicit Drug Use Disorder	7.1	2.6	32.9
Alcohol & Drug Use	2.6	0.9	12.1
Alcohol Only	14.4	5.4	66.9
Illicit drugs Only	4.5	1.7	20.9

Source: SAMHSA, 2015

Criminal Justice Context

It is evident that information about substance use, and particularly substance abuse disorders among justice-involved people, varies across studies. First, some studies provide data on substance involvement, while others address substance use disorder (i.e., under the influence of alcohol or other drugs at the time of their offense, stole money to buy drugs, were substance abusers, violated alcohol or drug laws, or share some combination of these characteristics). Second, some studies provide data on certain sectors of criminal justice like jails and prisons, while others are reporting results for persons arrested. Third, there are a few studies which are cited by subsequent studies. But, along the way other researchers are not citing the original study, but rather, they are citing the second-order authors who cited the original article. This gives the impression that numerous studies are providing substance abuse results.

We have tried to clarify the situation by the entries in Table 2-2. This table identifies the most often cited and most representative studies on substance use/abuse among prisoners. Further, we have provided type of results regardless of whether all the entries provide such measures. The five studies we have included do capture the state of our knowledge.

Table 2-2. Substance Use / Abuse: Prison and Jail Inmates

	Karberg and James 2005	Mumula and Karberg 2006	CASA 1998	CASA 2010	Bronson and Stroop 2017
Substance Involved	80%		80%	83.0%	
Substance Disorder	40%			64.5%	
Substance Use at Time of Crime	50%	State = 32% Federal = 26%	17%	20.0%	State = 42% Jail = 37%
Substance Abuse					
All Inmates	68%		78.6%	84.8%	
Federal		45%	80%	86.2%	
State		53%	81%	84.6%	58%
Jails	50%		73.4%	84.7%	63%

The National Center on Addiction and Substance Abuse (CASA) has published two studies that have provided very important findings about substance abuse and crime.

In the first study, CASA reported that in 1996, four out of five of America's 1.7 million prison and jail inmates were substance involved (CASA, 1998). The CASA report also indicated that the prevalence of drug involvement was high regardless of the prison venue. The percentage for inmates regardless of location was 78.6 percent, while the scores for specific categories were 81 percent for state prisons, 80 percent for federal prisons, and 73.4 percent for jails.

Second, CASA replicated the study in 2010 and found that the problem had increased between 1996 and 2006. Of the 2.3 million adults behind bars, 1.9 million (83%) were substance involved—an increase from the 80 percent in 1996. CASA's second study (2010) has also indicated that the substance abuse problem among inmates had also increased across all correctional venues: 84.8 percent of all inmates (1.9 million) were substance involved, 86.2 percent of federal inmates (200,00), 84.6 percent of state inmates (1.1 million) and 84.7 percent of local jail inmates (600,000). CASA's 1998 study did not have the data necessary to determine whether the inmates met the DSM-IV medical criteria for alcohol and other drug use disorder. The 2010 study did, however, and CASA found that almost two-thirds (64.5%) met the medical criteria for an alcohol or other drug use disorder.

Third, in both studies, CASA also found that a non-trivial percent of the inmates, regardless, of whether they met the DSM-IV medical criteria for alcohol and other drug abuse and addiction, were substance involved–that is, they were under the influence of alcohol or other drugs at the time of their offense, stole money to buy drugs, were substance abusers, violated alcohol or drug laws, or share some combination of these characteristics. The percentages were 17 percent in 1996 and 20 percent in 2006.

Between the two CASA studies, there were two Bureau of Justice Statistics report which corroborate the CASA results in significant respects. Karberg and James (2005, widely cited) found that 50 percent of jail inmates in 2002 were substance abusers. They also noted (like CASA) that 80 percent of jail inmates were substance involved and 40 percent had a substance use disorder. Similarly, Mumula and Karberg (2006) found that 45 percent of federal inmates and 53 percent of state inmates were substance abusers. These BJS studies also showed that substance abuse was proximate to the offense for which offenders were incarcerated. Karberg and James (2005) found that half of all convicted jail inmates were under the influence of drugs or alcohol at the time of offense and similarly, Mumola and Karberg (2006) found that almost one-third of state and one-quarter of federal prisoners committed their offense under the influence of drugs.

Begum, Early, and Hodge (2016) is the most recent Bureau of Justice Statistics study and it reports data on state inmates and jail prisoners. They found lower percentages of drug abuse than did either CASA study (state = 58%; jail = 63%). They did, however, find the highest percentages of drug involvement at the time of the offense (state = 42%; jail = 37%).

The Substance Abuse and Mental Health Services Administration (SAMHSA, 2011) compared cases admitted to probation or parole that had no prior substance abuse treatment episodes with those who had three or more prior treatment episodes. The latter were almost twice as likely to have reported primary cocaine abuse (19.4% vs. 11.0%), almost four times as likely to have reported primary heroin abuse (16.8% vs. 4.9%), and about half as likely to have reported primary marijuana abuse (17.5% vs. 30.0%). Further, data from a national study in five major American cities shows that at the time of arrest, 63 percent to 83 percent of arrestees had drugs in their system, with marijuana and cocaine being the most common and that between 2000 and 2013, the percentage of arrestees with opiates in their system increased, with a couple of cities seeing significant increases in opiate presence, as well as methamphetamine (Center for Prisoner Health and Human Rights, 2016).

Mental Health Disorders

General Population

As we did for substance abuse disorders, we provide data concerning the prevalence of mental health disorders in the general population. These data are a necessary baseline for any discussion of this issue among justice-involved persons. Table 2-3 provides the results from national data concerning behavioral health trends in the United States (from the 2014 National Survey on Drug Use and Health from the Center for Behavioral Health Statistics and Quality, the Substance Abuse and Mental Health Services Administration, SAMHSA, 2015). These data are the most recent and best source of information concerning national level estimates of mental health disorders. SAMHSA provides estimates of any mental illness (AMI) and serious mental illness (SMI) for adults aged 18 or older. An adult with AMI was defined as having any mental, behavioral, or emotional disorder in the past year that met DSM-IV criteria (excluding developmental disorders and SUDs). Adults with AMI were defined as having SMI if they had any mental, behavioral, or emotional disorder that substantially interfered with or limited one or more major life activities (SAMHSA, 2015: 28). Fortunately, the estimates of mental health disorders are considerably lower than was the case for substance abuse. SAMHSA found that in 2014, 43.6 million people, 18.1 percent of the general population, had a diagnosed mental illness. The prevalence drops to 4.1 percent (9.8 million people), for the prevalence of a serious mental illness.

Table 2-3. Mental Health Disorders in Adults: 2014

	Number in Millions	Percent of Population	Percent of AMI Pop.
Any Mental Illness (AMI)	43.6	18.1	100
Serious Mental Illness (SMI)	9.8	4.1	22.7
Any Mental Illness Only	33.7	14	77.3

Source: SAMHSA, 2015

Criminal Justice Context

Several studies have investigated the mental health deficits of offenders that can affect reentry and can lead to an increased risk of recidivism. Over time, these studies have provided strong evidence about the prevalence of mental illness among offenders. In one Bureau of Justice Statistics (BJS) study, Ditton (1999) has reported several findings of interest. First, 16 percent of state prison inmates, 7 percent of federal inmates, and 16 percent of those in local jails reported either a mental condition or an overnight stay in a mental hospital, while another 16 percent of probationers were found to have had a mental condition or stayed overnight in a mental hospital at some point in their lifetime. Second, state prison inmates with a mental condition were different than other inmates: (1) more likely than other inmates to be incarcerated for a violent offense (53% compared to 46%); (2) more likely than other inmates to be under the influence of alcohol or drugs at the time of the current offense (59% compared to 51%); and (3) more than twice as likely as other inmates to have been homeless in the 12 months prior to their arrest (20% compared to 9%). Third, the mental illness and crime connection appeared to be longstanding–over three-quarters of mentally ill inmates had been sentenced to time in prison or jail or on probation at least once prior to the current sentence.

In a second BJS study, James and Glaze (2006) investigated mental health problems that were defined by two measures: a recent history or symptoms of a mental health problem which occurred in the 12 months prior to the interview. A recent history of mental health problems included a clinical diagnosis or treatment by a mental health professional. Symptoms of a mental disorder was based on criteria specified in the Diagnostic and Statistical Manual of Mental Disorders, fourth edition (DSM-IV). They found that more 54 percent of all prison and jail inmates had a mental health problem, including 705,600 inmates in state prisons, 78,800 in Federal prisons, and 479 ,900 in local jails. These counts of mental illness cases represented 56 percent of state prisoners, 45 percent of federal prisoners, and 64 percent of jail inmates. Similarly, Steadman, Osher, Robbins, Case, and Samuels (2009) reported that 16.9 percent of people admitted to jail have serious mental illnesses and these rates are three times higher for men and six times higher for women than those found in the general population. An earlier study by Steadman, Fabisiak, Dvoskin, and Holohean (1989) found that only 8 percent of state jail inmates suffered from serious mental illnesses. The National Center on Addiction and Substance Abuse (2010) has reported a much higher percentage of mental illness–one-third (32.9 percent) of the 2.3 million prison and jail inmates. Other research has provided lower estimates of mental illness among offenders when precise diagnostic measures of mental health symptoms are used. These estimates of the prevalence of offenders with mental illness in jails and prisons range from 10 to 15 percent of criminal justice populations (Lamb, Weinberger, and Gross, 2004; Teplin, 1990; Teplin, 1994; Teplin, Abram, and McClelland, 1996).

Table 2-4. Mental Health Disorders in Prisons and Jails

Identified as Mentally Ill	Steadman et al. 1989	Teplin 1990	Dutton 1999	James and Gaze 2007	Steadman et al. 2009
State	8%		16.2%	56%	
Federal			7.4%	45%	
Jail		10%	16%	54%	16.9%
Probationers			16%		

Co-Occurring Disorders

General Population

The last risk factor is co-occurring disorders, the risk factor about which we have the greatest interest. As we did for substance abuse and mental health disorders, we provide national data concerning the estimated prevalence of the co-morbidity of substance abuse disorders and mental health disorders in the general population. Given the focus of this book–the association between co-occurring disorders and successful prisoner reentry–these data are a crucial baseline for any discussion of the likelihood of recidivism among the reentry population. Table 2-5 provides the results from national data concerning behavioral health trends in the United States (from the 2014 National Survey on Drug Use and Health from the Center for Behavioral Health Statistics and Quality, the Substance Abuse and Mental Health Services Administration, SAMHSA, 2015). These data are the most recent and best source of information concerning national level estimates of mental health disorders.

The SAMHSA data indicate that co-occurring disorders are rare. An estimated 7.9 million people, or just 3.3 percent of the general population has a diagnosed co-occurring disorder. It is also true that the prevalence of co-occurring disorders varies depending on which sub-population is examined. That is, among persons with a diagnosed substance abuse disorder, 36.7 percent have a co-occurring disorder. On the other hand, the prevalence of co-morbidity is half as high for persons with any mental illness (18.1%). SAMHSA indicated that these data are the same from 2008 through 2014.

Table 2-5. Co-Occurring Disorders in Adults: 2014

	Number in Millions	**Percent of Population**	**Percent of AMI**	**Percent of SUD**
Co-Occurring Disorders	7.9	3.3	18.1	36.7

Source: SAMHSA, 2015

Criminal Justice Context

The research on substance abuse and mental health disorders among offenders revealed that substance abusers also had significant prevalence of mental illness problems and vice versa. Thus, research started to investigate the co-morbidity of these risk factors. To the extent that a significant joint association could be determined, there would be a need for increased attention to these offenders while incarcerated, and more importantly, as factors that had to be addressed during reentry. Research began to investigate the co-occurrence of these phenomena. However, given the emerging importance of the topic of co-occurring disorders among offenders, one would expect that numerous published studies would provide estimates of the extent of the co-morbidity. Unfortunately, such is not the case. To the contrary, the majority of studies merely indicate that the co-morbidity of mental illnesses and substance use disorders is highly important and that the prevalence among offenders "far exceeds that of the general population," but no estimates of the extent of co-morbidity are actually provided (see, Baillargeon, Binswanger, Penn, Williams, and Murray, 2009a; Osher, Steadman, and Barr, 2003; Osher, 2013, Peters, Bartoi, and Sherman, 2008; Peters, Wexler, and Lurigio, 2015). This is very disappointing.

It is even more problematic when published studies provide a so-called estimate of co-morbidity–the percent of substance abuse disorders among offenders with mental health disorders, or the prevalence of mental disorders among offenders with a substance abuse disorder. Many studies fail to provide the underlying percentage of the first, when indicating the co-occurrence percentage. For example, Peters, Bartoi, and Sherman reported that, "Other studies indicate that 72–87 percent of justice-involved individuals with severe mental disorders have co-occurring substance use disorders" (2008: 2). The so-called 72-87 percent co-morbidity statistic is not only not helpful but can also be highly misleading. The issue is that, because Peters et al. (2008) do not provide the underlying percentage of the mental health disorders, we cannot determine co-morbidity. That is, if the mental disorder inmates constitute only 10 percent of justice-involved people, then co-morbidity represents only from 7.2 to 8.7 percent. If, however, 40 percent of the justice-involved individuals have diagnosed mental health disorders, then co-morbidity affects from 28.8 to 34.8 of the individuals. Simply, much prior research has failed to provide meaningful data concerning co-morbidity prevalence (Abram and Teplin, 1991; Abram, Teplin, and McClelland, 2003; Chiles, Cleve, Jemelka, and Trupin, 1990).

A related problem with the co-morbidity literature is that reference is made to the prevalence of co-morbidity, but yet, there is no supporting evidence. For example, a National Institute of Health *Fact Sheet* on addiction in the criminal justice system indicated as follows:

> "As in the general population, co-occurring substance use and other mental disorders are common, with about 45% of inmates in local jails and State

> prisons having both. In addition, about 75% of inmates with a mental illness also meet criteria for substance abuse, and vice-versa. This high rate of co-occurrence underscores the need for offenders, both adults and juveniles, suffering from one disorder to be screened for the other and, where appropriate, treated for both, necessitating an integrated treatment approach" (NIH: 2010).

The NIH fact sheet provides no data nor any references to support the 45 percent and 75 percent statistics. Further, we know with certainty that co-occurring disorders are not common in the general population. It is misleading, therefore, to categorize the problem as having a "high rate of occurrence." Fortunately, there are a few studies that have provided estimates of the co-morbidity of mental disorders and substance abuse among criminal offenders. Table 2-6 lists the four studies.

Table 2-6. Co-Occurring Disorders in Prisons and Jails

Inmate Group	Cote and Hodgins 1990	James and Gaze 2006	NIH 2010	Blandford and Osher 2013
State prison		10%		9.40%
Federal prison	5 - 74%	7%		
Jail		11%		12.2%
All prisons and jails			45%	
Probation / Parole				3.9%

Cote and Hodgins (1990) investigated co-occurring disorders in a random sample of 650 inmates in the penitentiaries in Quebec, Canada. The sample constituted 21.9 percent of the male penitentiary population in April 1988. Disorders were based on results from the Diagnostic Interview Schedule which uses DSM-III criteria but can be administered by lay interviewers. A variety of statistical results are reported for co-morbidity based on mental illness disorders and then drug abuse concurrence, or drug abuse diagnosis and then the co-occurrence of various mental health disorders. For our purposes, we will focus on the latter. Among the inmates determined to have a substance abuse diagnosis, the co-morbidity results for mental disorders were as follows: (1) schizophrenic disorders, 10.8 percent; (2) bipolar disorder, 5.4 percent; (3) atypical bipolar disorder, 5.4 percent; (4) major depression, 17.4 percent; (5) antisocial personality, 74.7 percent; and (5) alcohol abuse, 74.7 percent. For each co-morbidity category, the prevalence is far greater than in the general population.

James and Glaze (2006) analyzed the data from two Bureau of Justice Statistics (BJS) surveys: (1) Inmates in State and Federal Correctional Facilities, 2004; and (2) Inmates in Local Jails, 2002. BJS has conducted the surveys every 5 to 6 years since 1972 and these inmate surveys are the only national source of detailed information on criminal offenders, particularly special populations such as drug and alcohol users and offenders who have mental health problems (James and Glaze, 2006: 11). Among the many descriptive tables, the results of co-morbidity are relevant here. James and Glaze compared drug-involved inmates with and without mental health issues for state and federal prison inmates and local jail prisoners. They found that mental disorders affected 56.2 percent of state inmates, 44.8 percent of federal inmates, and 64.2 percent of jail prisoners. They also found that these impaired inmates also had abused drugs, 18 percent state, 16.1 percent federal, and 17.3 percent jails. When we combine these percentages to reflect co-morbidity, we see that mental health disorders occur with substance abuse issues for 10 percent of all state inmates, 7 percent of all federal inmates, and 11 percent of all prisoners in local jails. These data are far in excess of the general population situation.

Blandford and Osher (2013) have provided the most recent co-morbidity data. They estimated mental illness and drug abuse co-morbidity from a variety of sources. The sources cited came from different years, used different methodologies and definitions, and combined different data sets. According to Blandford and Osher, "the table is intended to give the reader a general sense of the prevalence rates of behavioral disorders in corrections populations and is not intended to be the definitive epidemiologic dataset" (2013: endnote 3, p.33). With the caveat duly noted, the table does provide highly valuable information. The estimated prevalence of serious mental disorders are as follows: 5.4 percent for the general public, 16 percent for state prisons, 17 percent for jails, and 7 to 9 percent for probation and parole cases. The prevalence of substance abuse across these categories, assuming a serious mental health condition are as follows: 25 percent for the general public, 59 percent for state prisons, 72 percent for jails, and 49 percent for probation and parole cases. As we did above, the correct co-morbidity prevalence is determined by multiplying the two percentages across the four categories.

Thus, the estimated co-morbidity of a serious mental illness combined with substance abuse is as follows: 1.4 percent for the general public, 9.4 percent for state prisons, 12.2 percent for jails, and 3.9 percent for probation and parole cases. Confidence in these estimates is enhanced because the general public co-morbidity figure of 1.4 percent is very close to 1.0 percent reported in the SAMHSA (2015) study. Based on the findings from this study, compared to the general public, co-morbidity was found to be 6.7 times higher among state prisoners, 8.7 times higher for jail prisoners, and 2.8 times higher for people on probation or parole.

Risk Factors Summary

Substance Use Disorders

This chapter reviewed the research literature concerning three major risk factors associated with criminal behavior. These factors are: (1) substance use disorders; (2) mental illness disorders: and (3) the co-occurrence of both of these two risk factors. There was substantial literature on the first two risk factors, but comparatively less on co-occurring disorders. For all three risk factors, the prevalence of these phenomena is considerably higher among criminals than is the case among the general public.

We reported extensive national data from the *National Survey on Drug Use and Health* from the Center for Behavioral Health Statistics and Quality, the Substance Abuse and Mental Health Services Administration (SAMHSA, 2015). These data indicated that among persons 12 years old and older, 21.5 million people, or 8.1 percent, were classified as having a substance use disorder (SUD). The results further showed that 17 million people (6.4%) had an alcohol use disorder, while 7.1 million people (2.6%) had an illicit drug use disorder.

However, we also cautioned that these percentage statistics are an undercount because children aged 12 through 17 are included in the data. If data were reported only for adults the percentages would be much higher. The criminal justice context of substance use disorders is extensive among criminals.

First, substantial proportions of offenders have diagnosed substance abuse issues. The most recent data from the Center for Substance Abuse (CASA) showed that of the 2.3 million adults behind bars, 1.9 million (83%) were substance involved which was an increase from the 80 percent in 1996. CASA's second study also indicated that the substance abuse problem among inmates had also increased across all correctional venues: 84.8 percent of all inmates (1.9 million) were substance involved, 86.2 percent of federal inmates (200,00), 84.6 percent of state inmates (1.1 million) and 84.7 percent of local jail inmates (600,000). CASA's data also found that almost two-thirds (64.5 percent) met the medical DSM-IV criteria for an alcohol or other drug use disorder.

Second, in all the studies reviewed, significant percentages of inmates, regardless of whether they met the DSM-IV medical criteria for alcohol and other drug abuse and addiction, were substance involved–that is, they were under the influence of alcohol or other drugs at the time of their offense, stole money to buy drugs, were substance abusers, violated alcohol or drug laws, or share some combination of these characteristics.

The two CASA studies were corroborated by two Bureau of Justice Statistics reports. Karberg and James (2005, widely cited) found that 50 percent of jail inmates in 2002 were substance abusers. They also noted (like CASA) that 80 percent of jail inmates were substance involved and 40 percent had a substance use disorder. Similarly, Mumula and Karberg (2006) found that 45 percent of federal inmates and 53 percent of state inmates were substance abusers.

Third, many criminals used drugs proximal to the time of their offenses, or they were under the influence of drugs at the time they were arrested.

Mental Health Disorders

The literature indicated that the prevalence estimates of mental health disorders are considerably lower than substance use disorders. The Substance Abuse and Mental Health Services Administration study reported that in 2014, 43.6 million people, 18.1 percent of the general population, had a diagnosed mental illness. The prevalence drops to 4.1 percent (9.8 million people) for the prevalence of a serious mental illness (SAMHSA, 2015). In the criminal justice system studies have generally indicated that about 16 percent of inmates have a diagnosed mental illness problem. On the high end, James and Gaze (2006) found that more than 54 percent of all prison and jail inmates had a mental health problem, including 56 percent of state prisoners, 45 percent of federal prisoners, and 64 percent of jail inmates.

Co-Occurring Disorders

The Substance Abuse and Mental Health Services Administration reported that co-occurring disorders are very rare. According to the study, an estimated 7.9 million people, or just 3.3 percent of the general population has a diagnosed co-occurring disorder (SAMHSA, 2015).

Our principal concern in this chapter was to summarize the results concerning the extent of co-occurring disorders among justice-involved persons. Despite the fact that numerous observers point out the importance of investigating co-occurring disorders, and that reentry is compromised because of these disorders, there is a paucity of definitive research. There are few studies which report the actual prevalence of co-occurring disorders. There are even fewer studies that report useable percentages. Realistically, there are only two studies (James and Gaze, 2006; Blandford and Osher, 2013) which provide adequate data on the underlying percentages of substance abuse disorders and mental illness disorders. These studies are in general agreement that co-occurring disorders affect between 7 percent and 12 percent of inmates across all the corrections venues. Suffice it to say, therefore, that a conservative estimate is that incarcerated offenders suffer from co-occurring disorders from two to four times as often as the general public. We suspect that this range is an underestimate but only further research will facilitate the resolution of the exact situation.

We suspect that the ratio is much higher but there are just insufficient data. One major reason for the lack of competent data is that we also suspect that the screening and assessment of co-occurring disorders is not happening in correctional settings to the extent that it should. This topic is examined in Chapter Three.

CHAPTER THREE

SCREENING, ASSESSMENT, AND TREATMENT

Given the strength of the relationship between co-occurring disorders and crime, it is obvious that effective screening and assessment should be a routine practice in correctional settings. Co-occurring disorders often go unnoticed by the criminal justice system, or only the substance abuse or the mental health problem is identified. As one can imagine, when significant disorders like substance abuse or mental health are not identified, and in particular, when these disorders co-occur and are not recognized, successful intervention is not possible. In fact, it is highly likely that when co-occurring disorders are not addressed simultaneously, this greatly exacerbates the risk factors for recidivism and can lead individuals back into the criminal justice system over and over again. While we know that co-occurring disorders are quite prevalent in correctional facilities, there has historically been little done to treat inmates for their specific needs because of the failure to screen and assess effectively persons with co-occurring disorders in the justice system (Chandler, Peters, Field, and Juliano-Bult, 2004).

In this chapter we will first cover a variety of issues surrounding screening and assessment including differentiating between screening and assessment, importance of screening and assessment, and barriers to screening and assessment. Thereafter, we will provide an inventory of screening and assessment instruments for co-occurring disorders.

Screening and Assessment Defined

Screening

Peters, Bartoi, and Sherman (2008) have provided the following overview of screening for co-occurring disorders in correctional settings: "Screening is a brief, routine process designed to identify indicators, or "red flags," for the presence of mental health and/or substance use issues that reflect an individual's need for treatment and for alternative types of supervision and/or placement in housing or institutional settings" (2008:

7). They have also indicated that an initial screening session may include a brief interview, use of self-report instruments, and a review of archival records. Brief self-report instruments are useful to capture easily documented psychiatric symptoms and patterns of substance abuse and related psychosocial problems (2008:7). According to Peters, Bartoi, and Sherman, the goals of screening are as follows:

- Detection of current mental health and substance use symptoms and behaviors;
- Determination as to whether current symptoms or behaviors are influenced by co-occurring disorders;
- Examination of cognitive deficits;
- Identification of violent tendencies or severe medical problems that may need immediate attention; and
- Determination of eligibility and suitability for specialized co-occurring disorders treatment services (2008: 7).

Assessment

By comparison, assessment is a much more comprehensive and intensive process. Peters, Bartoi, and Sherman have indicated that assessment is typically conducted through a clinical interview and may include a psychological, laboratory, or other testing, and compilation of collateral information from family, friends, and others close to the individual (2008: 8). Compared to the mere identification of possible problems through the screening process, assessment is expected to provide a comprehensive examination of psychosocial needs and problems, including the severity of mental and substance use disorders, conditions associated with the occurrence and maintenance of these disorders, problems affecting treatment, individual motivation for treatment, and areas for treatment interventions (2008: 8). Peters, Bartoi, and Sherman also stressed that assessment must be viewed as an ongoing process that often includes engagement, identification of strengths and weaknesses, examination of motivation and readiness for change, review of cultural and other environmental needs, diagnosis, and determination of the appropriate setting and intensity/scope of services necessary to address co-occurring disorders and related needs (2008: 8).

The differences between screening and assessment are quite evident when one specifies the goals of assessment. According to Peters, Bartoi, and Sherman the goals of assessment are as follows:

- Examination of the scope and severity of mental and substance use disorders, and conditions associated with the occurrence and maintenance of these disorders;
- Development of diagnoses according to formal classification systems (e.g., DSM-IV-TR);
- Identification of the full spectrum of psychosocial problems that may need to be addressed in treatment;
- Determination of the level of service needs related to mental and substance abuse problems;
- Identification of the level of motivation and readiness for treatment;
- Examination of individual strengths, areas of functional impairment, cultural and linguistic needs, and other environmental supports that are needed;
- Evaluation of risk for behavioral problems, violence, or recidivism that may affect placement in various institutional or community settings; and
- Provision of a foundation for treatment planning (2008: 8).

Peters, Bartoi, and Sherman have also pointed out what they have called an integrated or blended screening and assessment approach to be used to examine co-occurring disorders in the criminal justice system (2008: 9). They have suggested that, in the absence of specialized instruments to address both disorders, an integrated screening approach typically involves use of a combination of mental health and substance abuse instruments. They have also indicated that integrated screening and assessment approaches are associated with more favorable outcomes (2008: 9; see also Kofoed, Dania, Walsh, and Atkinson, 1986) and help to maximize the benefits of scarce treatment resources.

Importance of Screening and Assessment

Many individuals entering the criminal justice system are unaware that they have diagnosable issues that could be playing a part in their criminality. Screening allows for agents working within the criminal justice system to gain a broader picture of the needs of the inmates and identify whether or not s/he is suffering from co-occurring disorders. Screening occurs before an assessment, as it indicates whether or not an assessment is necessary. There are numerous screening instruments available (Peters, Bartoi, and Sherman, 2008; Braude and Miller, 2011), though they vary quite considerably in cost, length of instrument, application, necessary training, and validity/reliability. Correctional facilities can determine which tool would work best within their setting, as there are quite a few that exist.

According to Peters, Bartoi, and Sherman (2008: 7) screening should be conducted for all inmates shortly after entry to a prison or jail. Although there are separate screening instruments that have been developed to detect mental health and substance use issues in the criminal justice system, until recently few instruments were available for examining co-occurring disorders simultaneously. Thus, screening is conducted early in the process of compiling information, and the results inform the need for assessment and diagnosis (Drake and Mercer-McFadden, 1995).

However, screening is not enough. Assessments need to be done to capture the broader picture and turn it in to a specific plan of action for inmates based on the actuality of their issues rather than just the knowledge that the issues exist. Assessment enables the acquisition of more detailed information about the condition of the individual, which allows the determination of a proper diagnosis and the development of appropriate programming and treatment for each individual in the criminal justice setting. Much like screening instruments, there are many options for mental health issues or substance use, but few options for co-occurring disorders. Assessment, therefore, will better enable productive use of resources, placement, and discharge planning to ultimately reduce recidivism.

Screening and assessment can help to determine the relationship between co-occurring disorders and prior criminal behavior, and to identify the need for criminal justice supervision. Because of the high rates of co-occurring disorders in justice settings, detection of one type of disorder (i.e., either mental or substance use) should immediately "trigger" screening for the other type of disorder. In general, the presence of mental health symptoms is more likely to signal a substance use disorder than substance use symptoms to signal a mental disorder. If both mental and substance use disorders are present, the interaction of these disorders and motivation for treatment should be assessed (Peters, Bartoi, and Sherman, 2008: 9).

Peters, Bartoi, and Sherman have offered several important recommendations concerning the development of a comprehensive screening and assessment approach. Their recommendations include the following:

- All individuals entering the criminal justice system should be screened for mental and substance use disorders. Universal screenings are warranted due to the high rates of co-occurring disorders among individuals in the criminal justice system and to the negative consequences for non-detection of these disorders.

- Screening should be routinely conducted for history of trauma and abuse, particularly among female offenders who are affected disproportionately by these problems.

- Mental health and substance abuse screening should be completed at the earliest possible point after involvement in the criminal justice system. For example, identification of these problems among pretrial defendants will assist the judge to establish conditions of release (e.g., drug testing, involvement in treatment) that will increase the likelihood of stabilization in the community and of the individual's return for additional court hearings.

- Ongoing screening for co-occurring disorders should be provided at the different stages of criminal justice processing, such as diversion, admission to jail, pretrial and presentence hearings, sentencing, probation, admission to prison, parole or aftercare, and revocation hearings. Ongoing screening will help to identify individuals who are initially reluctant to discuss mental health or substance abuse problems, but who may become more receptive to involvement in treatment services over time. For example, some individuals may seek treatment after learning more about correctional program services; others may experience mental health symptoms while incarcerated and elect treatment.

- Whenever feasible, similar or standardized screening instruments for co-occurring disorders should be used across different justice settings, with information regarding the results shared among all settings involved. This approach promotes greater awareness of co-occurring disorders and needed treatment interventions and reduces unnecessary repetition of screening and assessment for individuals identified as having co-occurring disorders.

- Information from previously conducted screening and assessment should be communicated across different points in the criminal justice system. A systemic approach to information sharing is needed, including development of memoranda of understanding/agreement among agencies having contact with the offender at different linkage points (2008: 9).

Cognitive and Behavioral Impairment

Peters, Bartoi, and Sherman have also raised the issues of cognitive and behavioral impairment as a problematic aspect of co-occurring disorders and offender recidivism. They have suggested that screening and assessment can be useful in detecting key cognitive and behavioral features related to co-occurring disorders, which can influence the course of treatment and may inform the type and format of treatment provided (2008: 12). One area that they identified as typically receiving insufficient attention during screening and assessment of co-occurring disorders is cognitive and behavioral impairment related to psychosocial and interpersonal functioning. This functional impairment often affects the individual's ability to engage and effectively participate in treatment because impairment in interpersonal or social skills influences the ability to interact with treatment staff, supervision officers, and other treatment team members. Related areas of functional ability include reading and writing skills, and how the individual responds to confrontation or stress, manages unusual thoughts and impulses, and handles finances (2008: 12).

Of prime importance in the present context is that these areas of cognitive and behavioral impairment are not frequently examined through traditional mental health or substance abuse assessment instruments, and yet are often more important than diagnoses in predicting treatment outcome and identifying needed treatment interventions (Peters, Bartoi, and Sherman, 2008: 13). They have also pointed out that individuals with co-occurring disorders often have significant cognitive impairment, including deficits related to concentration and attention, verbal memory, and planning abilities or "executive functions" (2008: 13). Thus, in comparison to other offenders, those with co-occurring disorders are characterized by the following cognitive and behavioral impairments:

- Difficulties in comprehending, remembering, and integrating important information, such as guidelines regarding treatment and supervision;
- Lack of recognition of the consequences related to criminal behavior or violations of community supervision arrangements;
- Poor judgment (e.g., related to substance use, discontinuation of medication);
- Disorganization in major life activities (e.g., lack of structure in daily activities, lack of follow through with directives);
- Short attention span and difficulty concentrating for extended periods;
- Poor response to confrontation and stressful situations;
- Impairment in social functioning;
- Less motivation to engage in treatment activities (2008: 13).

The evidence is very conclusive that these cognitive and behavioral deficits are important to consider in the context of screening and assessment. Peters, Bartoi, and Sherman (2008: 13) have discussed a variety of reasons:

1. They may influence the accuracy of information obtained during screening and assessment. Thus, assessments may need to be administered in several sessions for individuals who have difficulty concentrating for sustained periods.
2. These deficits may affect the outcomes of treatment and supervision, and should be considered in determining the intensity, duration, and scope of treatment and supervision.

3. They may actually become the focus of treatment and supervision activities through interventions such as skills training and motivational enhancement activities.

Unfortunately, many of these complex areas of cognitive and behavioral functioning are not easily measured or assessed using traditional instruments. Assessment of these areas is most effectively accomplished over a period of time and through an approach that incorporates observation, interview of collateral sources, review of records, and use of specialized assessment instruments (Peters, Bartoi, and Sherman, 2008: 13).

Clearly, when screening and assessments are not done accurately, or at all, individuals are much more at risk for a number of consequences, including:

- Increased reliance on psychotropic medicine
- Missed opportunities for appropriate treatment or intervention
- Lack of discharge planning and referrals to appropriate services
- Continuity of symptoms
- Increased risk of recidivism (Chandler et al., 2004; Drake, Alterman, and Rosenberg, 1993; Osher et al., 2003; Peters et al., 2008; Teague, Schwab, and Drake, 1990).

Barriers to Effective Screening and Assessment

There are numerous barriers to effective screening and assessment of co-occurring disorders. In a comprehensive monograph on screening and assessment, Peters, Bartoi, and Sherman, (2008) have identified major barriers to effective screening. The first barrier concerns the screening process itself. There may be a failure to examine one or more components of the co-occurring disorders. Sometimes this is due to ineffective screening instruments, or inadequate staff training or, because there is a bifurcated mental health and substance abuse service systems that feature separate screening and assessment processes (Peters, Bartoi, and Sherman, 2008: v). A second factor concerns the difficulty in determining whether psychiatric symptoms are caused by recent substance abuse or reflect the presence of a mental disorder (Peters, Bartoi, and Sherman, 2008: v).

Peters, Bartoi, and Sherman have also addressed the problem concerning symptom interaction between co-occurring disorders. They have indicated that screening and assessment of co-occurring mental and substance use disorders are often rendered more difficult by symptom interactions, including symptom mimicking, masking, precipitation, and exacerbation. Thus, understanding these interactions is important in identifying issues that may contribute to substance use relapse, recurrence of mental health symptoms, or both. Ongoing observation of symptom interaction is often needed to provide diagnostic discrimination between various different mental and substance use disorders (2008: 20). They have outlined the following key issues (2008: 20):

- Use of alcohol and drugs can create mental health symptoms;
- Alcohol and drug use may precipitate or bring about the emergence of some mental disorders;
- Mental disorders can precipitate substance use disorders (most individuals with co-occurring disorders report that mental health symptoms preceded substance abuse);
- Mental health symptoms may be worsened by alcohol or drug use;
- Mental health symptoms or disorders are sometimes mimicked by the effects of alcohol and drug use (e.g., cocaine intoxication can cause auditory or visual hallucinations); and
- Alcohol and drug use may mask or hide mental health symptoms or disorders (e.g., alcohol intoxication may mask underlying symptoms of depression)

According to Peters, Bartoi, and Sherman the considerable symptom interaction between co-occurring disorders leads to difficulties in interpreting whether symptoms are related to mental illness or substance abuse. Moreover, justice-involved individuals with co-occurring disorders may have difficulty providing an accurate symptom history due to cognitive impairment, mental health symptoms, confusion regarding the effects of their substance use, and to the chronic nature of their alcohol and drug use. Furthermore, individuals may anticipate negative consequences related to self-disclosure of mental health or substance abuse symptoms. Alternatively, symptoms may be feigned or exaggerated if an individual believes that this will lead to more favorable placement or disposition. For example, individuals who are incarcerated may falsely report mental health symptoms to receive medication, housing in medical units, or contact with medical staff (2008: 20-21).

Regardless of the causes for the ineffective screening of inmates, there is a pervasive failure to screen effectively persons with co-occurring disorders in the justice system (Chandler, Peters, Field, and Juliano-Bult, 2004). A major consequence of this failure is that offenders with co-occurring disorders are not accorded treatment or they are placed in inappropriate treatment (e.g., in less intensive services than are needed), resulting in high rates of criminal recidivism following release (Peters, Bartoi, and Sherman, 2008). Peters et al. have concluded, therefore, the justice system is generally not equipped to address the multiple needs of this population, and few specialized treatment programs exist in jails, prisons, or community corrections settings that provide integrated mental health and substance abuse services (2004: v). Braude and Miller (2011) have also raised important issues about cross-discipline screening. They noted the historic territorial issues and disagreements among disciplines about which disorder is primary, or more serious, or whether one precipitated the other. When clients are caught in the middle of different or incomplete systems of care, they do not get effective help for their full range of needs (2011: 4). Moreover, the failure to resolve disciplinary differences precludes the implementation of integrated treatment–specialized interventions that work concurrently for both substance use and mental health recovery (Braude and Miller, 2011:5).

Reliability and Validity of Instruments

It is important to note that many institutions are utilizing instruments that do not have published data on reliability and validity. This can lead to ineffective screening or assessment and a failure to deliver proper services. Further, many of these tools were created for a specific population, whether it be males or females or substance users seeking treatment. It is unwise to use such tools on population for which they were not designed.

Sacks et al. (2007) did a validation study looking at the MHSF, GSS, COSDI-MD, and MINI-M and found that while they appear valid, they each work best for their specific focuses (gender, mental disorder, etc.). Fortunately, the validation was conducted using inmates admitted to substance abuse treatment programs, thus we know that these tools are employable for imprisoned individuals. To assess the usefulness for co-occurring disorders, Sacks et al. (2007) employed the Texas Christian University Drug Screen to determine the individual's substance use disorders.

Screening Instruments

Mental Health Screening Instruments

The screening instruments for mental health disorders are listed in Figure 3-1 and are described below.

Brief Jail Mental Health Screen (BJMHS)

BJMHS is a short tool that screens inmates for mental health disorders quickly. It takes approximately three minutes and the eight questions require simply yes or no responses. The instructions provide simple to understand guidelines for each section of the screen, as well as other comments to ensure the administrator does so appropriately. It was designed to provide correctional employees with information for appropriate booking and classifying inmates, but also to suggest further assessment. Steadman, Scott, Osher, Agnese, and Robbins (2005) validated the BJMHS as a useful screen for male inmates, though it is not quite as effective for female inmates. It is applauded for its shortness and free access by Policy Research Associates.

Brief Symptom Inventory (BSI)

BSI is a screening instrument that looks at psychological distress and psychiatric disorders. It is a short questionnaire consisting of 53 Likert scale statements. They are easily scored using answer sheets and answer keys (Derogatis, 1993). Peters et al. (2008) note the BSI is useful for evaluating progress and summarizing symptoms at a given point of time. The tool has been deemed reliable, valid, and useful for work with offenders (Houck and Loper, 2002; Royse and Drude, 2009; Zabora et al., 2001). BSI does come at a cost through Pearson Assessments.

Correctional Mental Health Screen (CMHS)

CMHS is a questionnaire consisting of yes/no questions that takes between three and five minutes. Individuals who answer yes more frequently than no ought to be sent for further assessment. This screening tool closely resembles the BJMHS but is a bit longer in length with twelve questions. The tool offers an easy to understand instruction guide for those administering the screen, including information on the type of referral to be made.

Jail Screening Assessment Tool (JSAT)

JSAT is a screening tool that was developed for use in correctional facilities. It requires a trained mental health professional to conduct the twenty-minute interview. While its primary focus is to determine mental health status, it does offer a few questions about substance use and abuse. It requires a knowledgeable, trained administrator to decipher the responses and determine if they are considered positive or negative. It is heavily reliant on a strong rapport between the client and the interviewer (Grisso, 2006).

The manual provides the necessary information to administer and interpret the responses, though it does leave the interpretation to the judgment of the interviewer (Nicholls, Roesch, Olley, Ogloff, and Hemphill, 2005).

Mental Health Screening Form-III (MHSF-III)

The MHSF-III (Carroll and McGinley, 2000) is a yes/no tool that addresses the individuals' mental health issues throughout their lifetime. Given its simplicity, this tool can be administered by an agent within the correctional facility or by the inmate himself/herself. The MHSF-III asks questions about the individual's life history with mental health problems and if any prior treatment was sought.

Ruiz, Peters, Sanchez, and Bates (2009) evaluated the MHSF-III and consider it "promising" for its use in jail settings when screening mental health disorders. It is important to realize that given its simplicity, and the tool notes it as well, that it is ideal that the results then get discussed with a professional.

Psychiatric Diagnostic Screening Questionnaire (PDSQ)

PDSQ screens for most common Axis I disorders with thirteen sub scales and indicts the overall severity of the psychopathology (Zimmerman, 2001; Perkey, Sinclair, Blais, Stein, Neal, Pierson, and Slavin-Mulford, 2018). The tool was created to be more succinct than some of the other tools, in fact, Zimmerman (2001) believes it can be done while individuals are sitting in a waiting room or at their leisure at home. While it can be administered quite easily, it does need to be interpreted and scored by a trained professional. Zimmerman and Mattia (2002) conducted several studies to establish the reliability and validity of the tool, but also to ensure its readability; since then, it has been validated by many other studies (Perkey et al., 2018).

Substance Use Screening Instruments

The screening instruments for substance use are listed in Figure 3-2 and are described below.

Dartmouth Assessment of Lifestyle Instruments (DALI)

DALI is an 18-question screening instrument that must be administered by a trained professional. It covers minimal substance abuse, specifically focusing on alcohol, cannabis, and cocaine, but missing out on an abundance of other substances. It contains yes/no responses, as well as "not applicable", "refused", or "don't know". The instrument contains scoring instructions for the administrator.

Drug Abuse Screening Test (DAST)

DAST is a screening instrument that covers only prescription, over the counter, and illicit drug use, but does not include alcohol. It looks at the past twelve months of the individual's life. At the bottom of the tool are the scoring instructions to help determine if the individual has a substance use disorder. It is a brief tool that does not take much time to administer or score. Skinner (1982) has since developed a shorter tool with just ten questions.

Simple Screening Instrument for Substance Abuse (SSI)

The SSI draws from existing instruments and has been deemed one of most effective and commonly used instruments for use with incarcerated individuals (Peters et al., 2000; Moore and Mears, 2003). Along with being brief, it is also free to access. The questions are designed to be answered with yes/no responses. Scoring is simple with points scored for yes responses; the more yes responses the more of a risk for substance abuse. Peters et al. (2008) found this tool to be one of the most effective screening tools for male inmates for substance use issues.

Substance Abuse Subtle Screening Inventory (SASSI)

SASSI was developed in 1985 (Miller) to determine the likelihood of substance use disorders. It has been revised four times since its development. It contains indirect and direct statements with true/false responses and Likert scale questions (Feldstein and Miller, 2007). One of the flaws with SASSI is the subtlety of the questionnaire, as more direct questioning appears to be more effective (Peters et al., 2008). While SASSI is used in a variety of capacities, it is considered one of the least useful screening tools when utilized with inmates of the instruments studied by Peters et al. (2008). Though, Lazowski (2016) posits that SASSI is a reliable and valid tool, even when used with correctional population.

Texas Christian University Drug Screen-V (TCUDS)

TCUDS-V is a free resource provided by Texas Christian University. It consists of seventeen questions, including yes/no, list of drugs used, and frequency of use. TCUDS has been deemed more accurate than SSI (Moore and Mears, 2003) and has been considered the best tool out there for screening inmates by Peters et al (2007). It addresses use for the previous year including frequency, treatment, dependence and motivation for treatment. TCUDS-V is available in English, Spanish, Russian, Simplified Chinese, Traditional Chinese, and Vietnamese. It can be easily downloaded at no cost.

Co-Occurring Disorders Screening Instruments

The screening instruments for co-occurring disorders are listed in Figure 3-3 and described below.

Behavior and Symptom Identification Scale (BASIS-24)

BASIS-24 is a validated and reliable tool used to screen individuals suffering for mental health and substance use disorders (Eisen, Gerena, Ranganathan, Esch, and Idiculla, 2006; Cameron, Cunningham, Crawford, Eagles, Eisen, Lawton, Naji and Hamilton, 2007). This tool, developed by McLean Hospital, is quite brief and asks questions easy to understand; it also contains an "about you" section that addresses the demographics of the person. It can be scored by the administrator or through the purchase of an online scoring mechanism. It should be known that while it is simple to administer, it is a brief screen and should be reviewed by a clinician to ensure more information is gathered about the client's full diagnosis.

Centre for Addiction and Mental Health - Concurrent Disorders Screener (CAMH-CDS)

CAMH-CDS is a screening tool administered to individuals to determine whether s/he is suffering from mental health and substance use disorders. It covers eleven Axis I disorders and all substance use disorders (Negrete, Collins, Turner, Skinner, 2004). The tool can be administered by anyone and is relatively simple to administer, though it has not been tested in correctional settings. CAMH-CDS is also easily scored, as the interview can be completed via the computer and results viewed immediately. Negrete et al. (2004) note that it has been validated for its use with addicted individuals in treatment.

Co-Occurring Disorders Screening Instrument for Mental Disorders (COSDI-MD)

COSDI-MD was derived from three mental health screeners and has been deemed favorable over the three it was derived from (Sacks, Melnick, Coen, Banks, Friedmann, Grella, and Knight, 2007). It contains six questions with yes/no responses and is quickly administered. Upon completion of the screen, the tallying of yes/no allows the administrator to determine if the individual needs further assessment.

Global Appraisal of Individual Needs (GAIN)

GAIN is available in a variety of different formats, though two are better suited for co-occurring disorders: GAIN-I and GAIN-Q3. The GAIN is a semi structured assessment tool that has been updated and revised five times. The GAIN-I is the lengthier of the instruments, though shorter versions exist including the GAIN-SS, which only takes five minutes. The GAIN-Q3 was developed for use in justice settings. The Q3 is broken down into nine categories that are considered risk factors for criminality, including school and work problems, physical health, stress, risk behaviors, mental health, substance use, and crime and violence. Peters, Bartoi, and Sherman (2008) note that the shorter scales of GAIN are excellent tools for the justice system because of their brevity. They also note that the GAIN-I looks at a ninety-day time frame, which is neglectful as many suffer from their disorders throughout their lifetime.

GAIN offers a validity report to identify any inconsistencies that exist within the items.

MINI International Neuropsychiatric Interview - Modified (MINI)

The MINI (Sheehan, Lecrubier, Sheehan, Amorim, Janavs, Weiller, Hergueta, Baker, and Dunbar, 1998) is an instrument that evaluates 17 Axis I psychiatric disorders through the completion of 120 questions. While this instrument claims that it covers co-occurring disorders, it only asks one question about alcohol use and one about substance use (Peters et al., 2008). The MINI has been tested and deemed valid and reliable (Peterson, Modin, Wahlstrom, Hammarberg, and Krakau, 2018).

Mental Health Assessment Instruments

The assessment instruments for mental illness disorders are listed in Figure 3-4 and described below.

Minnesota Multiphasic Personality Inventory - 2 (MMPI-2)

The MMPI-2 is an assessment tool focused on the psychopathology of adults and has been utilized in a variety of settings, including correctional facilities. The MMPI-2 is a revision with better predictors and rephrasing to better reflect the current times (Framingham, 2016). It covers a wide range of diagnoses through its inclusion of clinical scales. While it can be administered by anyone with results scored by the computer, it can only be interpreted by a trained psychologist. The MMPI-2 covers ten clinical scales in its 567 questions, including hypochondriasis, depression, hysteria, psychopathic deviancy, masculinity-femininity, paranoia, obsessive compulsive, schizophrenia, hypomania, and social introversion (Peters et al., 2008).The MMPI-2 has been validated an abundance of times and is one of the most utilized tools (Drayton, 2009) in the field, including in correctional settings (Megargee and Carbonnell, 1995).

Millón Clinical Multiaxial Inventory-III (MCMI-III)

The MCMI-III is an assessment tool for personality disorders and clinical syndromes from Axis I and Axis II of the DSM-IV. Framingham (2016) notes that the MCMI-III stands out amongst other assessment tools because of its brevity, theoretical framework, validity, and format. The MCMI-III offers a useful report allowing the reviewer to quickly assess which diagnoses may apply to the individual (Peters et al., 2008). The MCMI-III may not be ideal for correctional settings, as it is set at an eighth-grade reading level (Peters et al., 2008) and may underreport personality disorders (Retzlaff, Stoner, and Kleinsasser, 2002).

Personality Assessment Inventory (PAI)

The PAI was developed to offer information about psychopathology and to provide diagnosis and treatment. It has 344 items and has been translated into numerous languages. Morey (1998) developed the tool with a theoretical framework to ensure it encompasses the necessary items, including 22 scales with separate measures for ten disorders and indicates level of severity. The PAI needs to be administered and interpreted by a professional. This tool has been validated including in a correctional setting (Wang, Rogers, Giles, Diamond, Herrington-Wang, and Taylor, 1998; Edens and Ruiz, 2006).

Substance Use Assessment Instruments

The assessment instruments for substance use disorders are listed in Figure 3-5 and described below.

Timeline Followback (TLFB)

TLFB is an assessment tool that looks at substance use for seven days to two years prior to the administration of the questionnaire. It can be conducted through interview or self-report. Individuals completing the TLFB are asked about the frequency of use. It covers substances including alcohol, tobacco, marijuana, prescription medication, and other illicit substances. It requires the individual completing the assessment to mark the days s/he used substances and the amount of substances used. TLFB is accessible online for no cost and in numerous languages.

Co-Occurring Disorder Assessment Instruments

The assessment instruments for co-occurring disorders are listed in Figure 3-6 and described below.

Addiction Severity Index - Fifth Version (ASI-V5)

The ASI-V5 is a comprehensive tool that has been used for screening, assessing, and treatment planning, though it was created primarily for assessment. It covers seven risk/needs including alcohol and drug use, as well as a glimpse into the individual's psychiatric status, thus making it a questionable assessment for co-occurring disorders. Its primary focus is on the disruption of life because of substance use (Mohammed, Marican, Othman, Thurairajasingam, and Ali, 2017). The tool itself is very lengthy and requires training to administer and score. ASI-V5 is accessible for free from its developer, Treatment Research Institute. Peters et al (2000) note that other researchers have found this tool may not be the most reliable or valid when screening individuals with co-occurring disorders, particularly when the mental illness is severe.

Comprehensive Addiction and Psychological Evaluation (CAAPE)

The CAAPE is an assessment tool allows for diagnosing mental health and substance use disorders. It was created by Norman Hoffman (2000) and takes approximately 20-35 minutes to complete. It covers six Axis I and six Axis III DSM-IV conditions including substance use/abuse, OCD, psychosis, and several personality disorders. CAAPE comes with a summary page that allows you to see more clearly the substance use and mental health conditions of the individual(s).

CAAPE has been utilized in correctional settings and has been validated for use especially in said settings (Tracy and Carkin, 2016). It is praised for its brevity and minimal training required for interviewers (Gallagher, Penn, Brooks, and Feldman, 2006).

Psychiatric Research Interview for Substance and Mental Disorders (PRISM)

PRISM is a diagnostic tool that addresses both substance and mental disorders, particularly those on Axis I and Axis II of the DSM-IV. It is conducted as a semi-structured interview and takes approximately ninety minutes to three hours depending on the individual administering the tool. PRISM looks at current and past diagnoses, so it covers the lifetime of the individuals being screened. PRISM must be administered by a master's level clinician. PRISM was validated and deemed reliable (Hasin, Samet, Nunes, Meydan, Matseoane, and Waxman, 2006 and Torrens, Serrano,

Astals, Perez-Dominguez, and Martin-Santos, 2004), thus making it an acceptable tool for use.

Structured Clinical Interview for DSM-IV (SCID)

SCID is an interview-based assessment tool that allows for diagnosis of DSM-IV diagnoses. It is considered one of the most widely used instruments (Peters et al., 2008). There are multiple versions that vary based on the number and type of DSM-IV diagnoses addressed. The questions can be tailored to be best understood by the clients but must be asked by an experienced, trained professional. SCID has been used in correctional settings (First et al., 2001; Peters et al., 1998).

Treatment of Co-Occurring Disorders

Given the complexity in the screening and assessment processes established in the previous sections, it is not hard to imagine the difficulties surrounding the treatment of co-occurring disorders inside correctional facilities, especially when these disorders are longstanding and have become chronic. We are not clinicians; we are researchers. Thus, we make no claims concerning either the appropriateness of, or the effectiveness of, particular treatment modalities. It would be irresponsible for us to do so. Instead, we conclude this chapter by providing the reader with a glimpse into what clinicians have indicated are likely to be best practice treatment approaches.

Braude and Miller (2011) have provided a comprehensive monograph on "understanding co-occurring disorders and applying integrated treatment strategies for adult correctional populations." Therein they indicate that there are two primary principles regarding treatment planning for inmates with co-occurring disorders which apply regardless of the treatment strategy: the dosage principle and pre-release planning 2011: 32. After these two principles are discussed, this section provides examples of evidence-based treatment models for inmates and other offenders with CODs.

First, they indicate that the effectiveness of any strategy is dependent on whether it has been administered appropriately and for sufficient time to kick in and produce an impact. They call this the "dosage principle." They argue that this is especially relevant for inmates with co-occurring disorders who have greater needs and pose a higher risk for relapsing and reoffending. They claim that long term programs, such as residential substance abuse treatment (RSAT) are much more effective, especially when they are followed up with services in the community upon release. We know the longer the individual stays engaged with treatment and recovery support, the better his or her chances of recovery are. Higher-risk offenders require significantly more structure and services than lower-risk offenders (2011: 32).

To bolster their argument, Braude and Miller provide data which showed that treatment for offenders with co-occurring disorders should be six months or longer whenever possible because new research on the threshold of cognitive behavioral therapy required to bring about change in high risk offenders indicates a minimum of 300 hours of cognitive-based interventions delivered over a period of 6-12 months is required (2011: 32).

Second, they identified the importance of pre-release planning. Regardless of the treatment approach while individuals are incarcerated, release planning should begin the day the treatment plan is developed. Many resources have long waiting lists and eligibility requirements that involve complicated paperwork, especially for offenders, who are typically not priority clients (2011: 33). Clearly, this issue speaks to the idea that planning for treatment leading to community reentry must begin very early during incarceration.

Braude and Miller have also provided information concerning a number of approaches that are deemed effective for offenders with both substance use and mental health disorders. The premise of all these strategies is to change motivation, attitudes, thinking and behaviors (2011: 33).

Cognitive Behavioral Therapy

The first approach is cognitive behavioral therapy (CBT). According to Braude and Miller (2011: 33) the cognitive behavioral approach targets a person's attitudes and thought processes, teaches individuals to recognize their thinking errors and to replace them with rational, pro-social thoughts. Practices like role plays, skill rehearsal and reinforcement allow individuals to try out new behaviors. Research on cognitive behavioral treatment in both the behavioral health and the correctional literature has demonstrated its effectiveness in prison and jail settings at not only reducing recidivism, but also in treating substance use and mental health problems.

Braude and Miller stress that, unlike many other approaches to psychotherapy, CBT emphasizes the idea of personal responsibility, while ensuring clients are provided with the coping and problem-solving skills they will need to succeed in everyday life. CBT focuses on the present rather than the past. CBT first concentrates on developing skills to recognize distorted or unrealistic thinking when it happens, and then to changing that thinking or belief to alter the negative behavior that contributed to justice involvement, such as continued substance misuse (2011:34). They also emphasize that most CBT programs are offered in small group settings and incorporate lessons and exercises involving role play, modeling or demonstrations. Further, individual counseling sessions are often part of CBT and clients are given homework and conduct experiments between sessions. These components are used to gauge the individual's readiness for change and foster engagement in that change. A willingness to change is necessary for CBT or any other treatment to be effective in reducing further criminal behavior (2011:34).

Braude and Miller provided an example of a brand name program, Thinking for a Change (T4C), which is a free program from the National Institute of Corrections for correctional agencies. Thinking for a Change requires 20-30 sessions which last for a period of up to 20 weeks. The rationale is that the more treatment provided or the more sessions participants attend over time, the greater the impact on and decrease in recidivism (2011:34).

Modified Therapeutic Community

Braude and Miller are positive on the merits of what is called a modified therapeutic community (MTC). MTC is a comprehensive treatment model that makes three key alterations for individuals with co-occurring disorders: it is more flexible, less intense, and more individualized 2011: 43). Braude and Miller indicate that, like all treatment community programs, MTC seeks to develop a culture where clients learn through a self-help process to foster change in themselves and others, and where the community becomes the healing agent. The major difference between a modified treatment community and a traditional treatment community is that an MTC is an integrated residential treatment program with a specific focus on public safety outcomes for persons with co-occurring disorders. Thus, according to Braude and Miller, the MTC is a derivative of the therapeutic community and has demonstrated lower rates of re-incarceration and a reduction in criminal activity among MTC participants (2011: 43). According to Braude and Miller, the MTC has several core principles and methods that are especially relevant to the treatment of co-occurring disorders:

- Providing a highly structured daily regimen;

- Fostering personal responsibility and self-help in managing life difficulties;

- Using peers as role models and guides with the peer community acting as the healing agent within a strategy of "community-as-method" (the community provides both the context for and mechanism of change);

- Regarding change as a gradual, developmental process and moving clients through progressive treatment stages; and

- Stressing work and self-reliance through the development of vocational and independent living skills; and promoting pro-social values within healthy social networks to sustain recovery (2011: 43).

Braude and Miller stress that MTCs include a community treatment element in their recovery approach. The objective is to treat the underlying substance abuse issues, which are related to continued criminal activity. By addressing the addiction problems of offenders while dealing with mental health disorders at the same time, MTCs aim to prevent future drug use and offending and reduce recidivism. The program benefits: (1) the offender by controlling substance use and providing treatment for mental health disorders; (2) the public by reducing future offending; and (3) the criminal justice (and health care) system by reducing the number of the offender's future interactions (2011: 43-44). These features are in contrast to the standard treatment community approach. As compared to the standard TC approach, the MTC:

- Incorporates increased flexibility;
- Reduces the duration of various activities;
- Reduces confrontation;
- Increases emphasis on orientation and instruction;
- Has fewer sanctions;
- Gives more explicit affirmation for achievements;
- Has greater sensitivity to individual differences; and
- Has greater responsiveness to the special developmental needs of the clients (2011: 44).

Braude and Miller believe that all of these features serve to maximize social learning opportunities by requiring all participants to have strong involvement and input into the "community" in order to feel involved and responsible. Staff members act as role models and steer the community members toward gaining greater control over their lives, their disorders, and their opportunities upon reentry. The MTC requires the involvement of treatment specialists, therapists and psychiatric services, group managers, program directors, and correctional security personnel. Key elements of the program include group therapy, individual therapy, monitoring of mental health, and medication management (2011: 44). Braude and Miller are also note that the above elements are linked to recovery stages in four phases and these phases are crucial:

- Phase 1: Admission and Orientation.
- Phase 2: Primary Treatment.
- Phase 3: Live-in Reentry.
- Phase 4: Live-out Reentry.

Braude and Miller could not stress any more strongly the following. In the best-case scenario, upon release from custody, inmates should continue treatment in the community for up to six months in a recovery home program. The program helps inmates continue the treatment that began while in prison, including examination and alteration of criminal thinking and behavior, mastering community living and integrating with society, gaining employment, and fostering connections with a larger recovery community.

Conclusion

This chapter has reviewed the screening and assessment instruments for substance abuse, mental illness, and co-occurring disorders. There are numerous tools available with varying characteristics. While there are obviously fewer tools available specifically geared toward co-occurring disorders, it is possible to combine a mental health instrument and a substance use instrument to achieve the same effect. TCUDS has been deemed the most effective tool for determining substance abuse, while GAIN-SS and MHSF-III were deemed accurate for mental health (Peters, Bartoi, and Sherman, 2008; webinar).

The literature indicated, of course, that screening is just the first step in providing a proper pathway toward recovery. Ideally, after being screened, individuals identified as suffering from co-occurring disorders will be further assessed via proper assessment tools. Thus, screening alone really is not sufficient and the assessment of inmates to fully diagnose and understand the extent of their issues is preferred.

To reduce recidivism, but also to aid in the recovery of inmates, the tools need to be utilized to guide the discharge plan and reentry services. They cannot merely be an "aha, I knew it" tool or simply used to designate a living space for inmates. Screening and assessment should be done on a continuous basis to verify that the needs of the inmates are being met and that the diagnoses are, in fact, correct. At a minimum, assessment should occur at intake, and before release.

We also briefly reviewed a few promising treatment programs for co-occurring disorders. Programs like cognitive behavioral therapy and modified treatment communities are reflected in a growing body of research as best practices for co-occurring disorders.

Figure 3-1. Mental Health Screening Instruments

Instrument	Number of Items	Scoring	Administered By	How Administered	Time to Administer	Year Created
Brief Jail Mental Health Screen (BJMHS)	8	Yes/No	Anyone	Interview	3 Minutes	2005
Brief Symptom Inventory (BSI)	53	Likert	Anyone	Self-report or Interview	8-10 Minutes	1993
Correctional Mental Health Screen (CMHS)	12	Yes/No	Anyone	Interview	3-5 Minutes	N/A
Jail Screening Assessment Tool (JSAT)	24	+/-	Trained Staff	Self-report or Interview	20-30 Minutes	2002
Mental Health Screening Form-III (MHSF-III)	18	Yes/No Frequency	Anyone	Self-report or Interview	15 Minutes	2000
Psychiatric Diagnostic Screening Questionnaire (PDSQ)	125	Yes/No	Anyone	Self-report	15-20 Minutes	2001

Figure 3-2. Screening Instruments for Substance Use

Instrument	**Number of Items**	**Scoring**	**Administered By**	**How Administered**	**Time to Administer**	**Year Created**
Dartmouth Assessment of Lifestyle Instrument (DALI)	18	Yes/No	Anyone	Interview	6 Minutes	1998
Drug Use Screening Test (DAST)	28	Yes/No	Anyone	Self-report	5-10 Minutes	1982
Simple Screening Instruments (SSI)	16	Yes/No	Anyone	Self-report or Interview	5-10 Minutes	1994
Substance Abuse Subtle Screening Inventory (SASSI)*	93	True/False	Anyone	Self-report	10-15 Minutes	1985
Texas Christian University Drug Screen-V (TCUDS)	15	Yes/No	Anyone	Self-report	5-10 Minutes	2007

Figure 3-3. Screening Instruments for Co-Occurring Disorders

Instrument	Number of Items	Scoring	Administered By	How Administered	Time to Administer	Year Created
Behavior and Symptom Identification Scale (BASIS-24)	24	Likert	Anyone	Self-report or interview	5-15 Minutes	2004
Centre for Addiction and Mental Health-Concurrent Disorders Screener (CAMH-CDS)	>24	Yes/No	Anyone	Self-report	5-20 Minutes	Unknown
Co-Occurring Disorders Screening Instrument for Mental Disorders (COSDI-MD)	6	Yes/No	Anyone	Interview	5-10 Minutes	2007
Global Appraisal of Individual Needs-I (GAIN-I)	1606	Yes/No	Trained Staff	Interview	120 Minutes	1993-1995
Global Appraisal of Individual Needs-Q3 (GAIN-Q3)	4-10 items per section; total 9 sections	Yes/No	Trained Staff	Interview	25-35 Minutes	1993-1995

Global Appraisal of Individual Needs-SS (GAIN-SS)	23	Yes/No	Trained Staff	Interview	5-10 Minutes	1993-1995
MINI International Neuropsychiatric Interview Modified (MINI)	120	Yes/No	Brief Training Required	Interview	15-20 Minutes	1992
Jail Screening Assessment Tool (JSAT)	N/A	N/A	Trained staff	Interview	20 Minutes	2005

Figure 3-4. Assessment Instruments for Mental Health

Instrument	Number of Items	Scoring	Administered By	How Administered	Time to Administer	Year Created
Minnesota Multiphasic Personality Inventory-2 (MMPI-2)	567	True False	Anyone	Self-report	60-90 Minutes	1989
Millon Clinical Multiaxial Inventory-III (MCMI-III)	175	True False	Psychologist	Self-report	30 Minutes	1994
Personality Assessment Inventory (PAI)	344	True False	Psychologists	Self-report	50-60 Minutes	1991

Figure 3-5. Assessment Instruments for Substance Use

Instrument	Number of Items	Scoring	Administered By	How Administered	Time to Administer	Year Created
Timeline Follow back	Calendar	Yes/No and Count	Anyone	Self-report or Interview	10-30 Minutes	1996

Figure 3-6. Assessment Instruments for Co-Occurring Disorders

Instrument	Number of Items	Scoring	Administered By	How Administered	Time to Administer	Year Created
Addiction Severity Index - Drug Use (ASI)	155	Likert	Trained Staff	Structured Interview	45-90 Minutes	1992
CAAPE	141	Yes/No	Anyone	Interview	25-30 Minutes	2000
Psychiatric Research Interview for Substance and Mental Disorders (PRISM)	Many	Yes/No	Trained Staff or Masters' Level Clinician	Semi-structured Interview	90 Minutes to 3 Hours	1996
Structured Clinical Interview for DSM-IV (SCID)	Varies Based on Answers	Yes/No	Trained Staff	Interview	45-120 Minutes	2015

CHAPTER FOUR

EXPERIMENTAL STUDY: DATA AND METHODS

As noted in Chapter One, this study resulted from a partnership between the School of Criminology and Justice Studies, University of Massachusetts Lowell, and the Essex County, Massachusetts, Sheriff's Department. We served as the research partner, a function which is mandated by the *Second Chance Act*. ECSD) to conduct an evaluation of ECSD's program for Adult Offenders with Co-occurring Disorders through funding from the Bureau of Justice Assistance's *Second Chance Act Reentry Program for Adult Offenders with Co-Occurring Substance Abuse and Mental Health Disorders* solicitation (BJA-2014-3773). The BJA solicitation indicated the following two principles. First, the Reentry Program for Adult Offenders with Co-Occurring Substance Abuse and Mental Health Disorders is designed to improve outcomes for adults with co-occurring substance abuse and mental health disorders through the screening and assessment of incarcerated individuals, availability of some pre-release programming, leading to the provision of appropriate evidence-based services and treatment after incarceration (BJA: p. 4). Second, BJA recognizes that a significant number of individuals who are incarcerated and returning to the community have chronic substance abuse and mental health disorders and need treatment in order to successfully complete their supervision, reduce recidivism, and promote public safety. The coordination of substance abuse and mental health treatment with correctional planning can encourage participation in treatment and can help treatment providers incorporate correctional requirements as treatment goals (BJA: p.5).

The Essex County Sheriff's Department originally proposed a community reentry program to address the institutional treatment and post-release transition back into the community of male inmates who were part of its Treatment and Recovery from Addictions in Corrections (TRAC) program. This target population was expected to exhibit continued criminogenic factors despite the excellent track record of the TRAC program owing to the following factors:

- Behavior attributable to currently untreated Co-Occurring Disorders (COD).
- High-risk for disciplinary actions and recidivism.
- Extensive criminal records.
- Weak or non-existent family support systems.
- Sporadic work experience and income gained primarily only illegally.
- Have no more than a high school education, unstable housing, and are substance abusers with sentences longer than six months.
- COD inmates represent one-third of offenders with substance abuse issues who enter the TRAC Program.
- COD inmates represent a growing segment of the ECSD corrections population and account for a disproportionate number of disciplinary issues.

The Essex County COD program was designed to address the following goals.

1. Increase the screening and assessment that takes place during incarceration as well as improve the provision of treatment to adults with co-occurring substance abuse and mental health disorders after incarceration.
2. Reduce the use of alcohol and other drugs by long-term substance abusers with co-occurring disorders during and after the transition from incarceration to the community, in order to reduce recidivism among program participants.
3. Improve outcomes for individuals with co-occurring substance abuse and mental health disorders through the provision of appropriate evidence-based services including addressing individual criminogenic needs.

4. Implement a reentry plan that relies on a risk and needs assessment that reflects the risk of recidivism for that individual.

We determined that the best research design would involve two components. First, an *outcome evaluation* would document the extent to which ECSD's COD program achieved the desired effects. In the present context, this concerns the extent to which the COD program did in fact result in: (1) evidence-based screening of CODs: (2) identification and provision of community reentry services; and (3) lower recidivism. Second, the evaluation should also include a process evaluation. Process analyses are often neglected in evaluation research studies. This is unfortunate because this type of evaluation research can generate findings that provide important feedback concerning service delivery itself. The present process analysis monitors program activities, but instead of inmate reentry/recidivism being the ultimate outcome measure, the process evaluation focused on various measures of program participation and fidelity and measured the consistency and successful implementation of the program separate and apart from outcomes.

Thus, the two components of the evaluation functioned together to ensure the ability of the evaluation to identify best practices. The usual outcome analyses are of course significant. After all, the ultimate purpose of the COD Program is to deliver more effective treatment to inmates thus leading to reduced recidivism Clearly, however, an evaluation should not focus disproportionately, and certainly not exclusively, on outcome measures per se, and neglect program implementation features. By ignoring a process analysis, the capacity of the evaluation to yield information is diminished concerning how and why ECSD might have been able to achieve comparatively better success rates than it has in the past. The design is superior to the usual outcome evaluation and provides much greater opportunity for achieving an outcome assessment while at the same time providing important contextual data concerning program participation and delivery.

Outcome Evaluation Design

Although a randomized experiment is very uncommon in correctional settings, ECSD agreed to let us conduct an actual experiment as indicated below.

Pre-Test Post-Test Control Group Design

R Experimental Ot1 X Ot2
R Control Oc1 Oc2

Where "O" signifies either an observation or measurement. Subscripts "t" or "c" refer to experimental vs. control groups. Subscripts "1" and "2" indicate the order of the measurement. "X" indicates occurrence of a treatment, activity, program, etc. while "R" indicates random assignment. This design uses random assignment to experimental and control groups to assess the impact of the treatment. With this design, one computes two change scores: one for the experimental group which equals O_{t2} - O_{t1}; and another for the control group which equals O_{c2} - O_{c1}. There are no methodological weaknesses with this design. Thus, a pre-test post-test control group design is the most rigorous evaluation research. While the specific requirements of the design make it typically very difficult to implement and very rare to find in criminal justice evaluation it is very rigorous. The structure of the design guards against all threats to internal validity thus ensuring that the post- test findings are directly attributable to the project activities being evaluated. The problems surrounding observed outcomes to implemented activities is very complicated because of the multi- faceted nature of the criminal justice system and the number and complexity of the confounding factors which may affect its operations. The design used here permits the unambiguous attribution of observed changes to the project.

Subject Selection and Assignment

ECSD inmates were selected for the project as follows. First, inmates were randomly selected for participation and were subsequently assessed for co-occurring disorders as described below. There were 201 inmates who were assessed for co-occurring disorders. If a co-occurring diagnosis was achieved, the inmate was eligible for the program. Among the 201 cases, there were 184 cases (91.5%) who were classified as having a co-occurring disorder. As Essex County expected, the prevalence of co-occurring disorders was quite high. There were 17 cases that were not determined to be suffering from a co-occurring disorder. See Table 4-1. Second, 92 of the 184 cases were then randomly assigned to both the experimental and control groups. Ultimately, there were 170 inmates across both conditions available for analysis because 14 experimental group cases were not released as originally scheduled owing to unresolved infractions. Because their release was delayed, they would have had much shorter periods at risk for recidivism after reentry. The final cases thus consisted of control (n=92) and experimental (n=78).

Measurement of Co-Occurring Disorders

Clinicians made the diagnosis of co-occurring disorders by using the Comprehensive Addictions and Psychological Evaluation (CAAPE). The Comprehensive Addictions and Psychological Evaluation (CAAPE) is screening instrument specifically designed to assess persons with co-occurring disorders (Hoffmann, 2000). The CAAPE provides detailed indications for abuse or dependence for nine substance categories (alcohol, marijuana, cocaine, heroin, stimulants, sedatives, hallucinogens, inhalants, and a category for mixed substance abuse). The CAAPE also covers six Axis I and six Axis II DSM-IV conditions–the more prevalent mental health conditions likely to impact recovery from substance use disorders. The CAAPE has been applied to adjudicated adolescents in secure facilities (Abrantes, Hoffmann, and Anton, 2005) and in a comparative analysis of the relative prevalence of substance use disorders among prison inmates in the United Kingdom and the United States (Jones and Hoffman, 2006). In the context of an evaluation of an integrated day treatment program for co-occurring disorders, research participants were interviewed using the structured clinical interview for DSM-IV (SCID) and the CAAPE (Gallagher, Penn, Brooks, and Feldman, 2006). We are not aware that there have been any peer-reviewed validation studies of the CAAPE. Thus, the present study is a first effort to examine the CAAPE's validity among a large sample of jail inmates.

Table 4-1. Results of Co-Occurring Disorders Screening

All Cases	COD	Not COD	Total
Number	184	17	201
Percent	91.5%	8.5%	100.00%
Not COD	**Neither**	**SUD Only**	**MH Only**
Number	6	8	3
Percent	3.0%	4.0%	1.5%

Variables

CAAPE Variables

Drug Abuse

The CAAPE employs a clinician-scored drug abuse scale that identifies four abuse levels: None, Mild, Moderate, and Severe which are scored from 0 to 3 for each of nine drugs (Alcohol, Marijuana, Cocaine, Stimulants, Sedatives, Heroin, Hallucinogens, Inhalants, and Mixed). In addition to these nine drug scales, we also calculated the following:

1. ***Total Drug Abuse Score*** (range = 1-27);
2. ***Number of Drugs Abused*** (count of any of the nine scale scores greater or equal to 1; range = 1-9); and
3. ***Number of Drugs Severely Abused*** (any of the nine scale scores equal to 3; range = 0-9).

Mental Health

The CAAPE provides three mental health measures.

The following nine disorders are scored dichotomously (Major Depressive, Manic, Panic, Post Traumatic Stress, Anxiety, Obsessive/ Compulsive, Psychosis, Anti-Social Personality, and Personality Disorder). The nine items are then evaluated to produce an overall ***Mental Health Score*** which ranges from 1 to 3 (Mild, Moderate, and Severe). The ***Number of Disorder Types*** is a count of the presence of the nine disorders (range 1 to 9).

As part of this research, we had to conduct a validation study of the CAAPE (Tracy and Carkin, 2017). Therein, we investigated the criterion validity of the CAAPE which represents the association between measures that are purportedly related. In psychometrics, criterion (or concrete validity) is the extent to which a measure is related to an outcome of interest. In the present case, if co-occurring disorders are related to criminal conduct, and if the CAAPE provides sufficient diagnosis of co-occurring disorders through the various scales and summary variables, then the CAAPE measures should serve as significant predictors of prior criminal history of the subjects in this study. Criterion validity is often divided into concurrent and predictive validity. Concurrent validity refers to a comparison between the measure in question and an outcome assessed at the same time, which here would be prior criminal history. Subsequently, the CAAPE scores should also have predictive validity–the extent to which the CAAPE explains post-release recidivism. Our research indicated that the CAAPE was a significant predictor of the prior criminal history of the subjects in this experimental program.

Prior Criminal History

- Arrests: count of the number of arrests prior to the current incarceration.
- Convictions: count of the total number of charges for which the subject was convicted prior to the current incarceration.

Reentry Recidivism

- Recidivism status is any post-release infraction (i.e., technical violation, arrest, or conviction).
- Count of arrests post-release.
- Count of convictions post-release.

Demographic Factors

- Race: coded as Other vs. White.
- Years of school completed.
- Marital Status: Single vs. ever married.
- Age in years at intake.

Group Composition

The paramount issue at this juncture concerns whether the control and experimental groups were statistically equivalent. Simply, did random assignment work as expected and produce two groups that did not have statistically significant differences across background factors, criminal history, and co-occurring disorder scores which would confound the comparisons between the experimental and control groups on the outcome measures. These comparison data are presented in the following tables.

Demographic Factors

Table 4-2 provides a breakdown of the race/ethnicity of the subjects. The control group is more likely to contain white subjects, while the experimental group has a higher percentage of African American and

Hispanic subjects, but these differences were not statistically significant based on a chi-square test of independence.

Table 4-3 shows the distribution of the marital status variable. Although the experimental group had a higher percentage of single subjects, and the control group had a higher percentage of people who were or had been married, the chi-square test indicated that the differences were not significant.

Table 4-4 provides data for three quantitative demographic variables for which t-tests were conducted. These data indicate that the experimental group is significantly better educated by a factor of about one-half grade level and is also about one and one-half years younger, but these differences were not statistically significant.

Criminal History Measures

Table 4-5 shows slight differences for four criminal history measures, but none were statistically significant. Table 4.6 shows the offense type for which the subjects had been incarcerated. The experimental group had substantially more drug offenders, while the control group had a slightly higher percentage of property offenders. These differences were not significant.

Table 4-2. Race/Ethnicity of Subjects

	Control	Experimental	Total
White	49	37	86
	53.3%	47.4%	50.6%
African American	7	9	16
	7.6%	11.5%	9.4%
Hispanic	33	30	63
	35.9%	38.5%	37.1%
Other	3	2	5
	3.3%	2.6%	2.9%
Total	92	78	170
	100.0%	100.0%	100.0%
	Not Statistically Different		

Table 4-3. Marital Status

	Control	Experimental	Total
Single	72	67	139
	78.3%	85.9%	81.8%
Ever Married	20	11	31
	21.7%	14.1%	18.2%
Total	92	78	170
	100.0%	100.0%	100.0%
	Not Statistically Different		

Table 4-4. Mean Years of School Completed, Age at Intake, and Age at Release

	Highest Grade	Age at Intake	Age at Release
Control	11.05	33.86	34.42
Experimental	11.69	32.34	32.76
Total	11.35	33.16	33.66
Significance	**Yes**	No	No

Table 4-5. Mean Criminal History Measures

	Time Served	Prior Arrests	Prior Convictions	Commitment Offense Scale
Control	5.6	16.01	15.47	4.35
Experimental	4.31	14.37	15.08	4.49
Total	5.01	15.26	15.29	4.41
Significance	No	No	No	No

Table 4-6. Commitment Offense

	Control	Experimental	Total
Violence	26	22	48
	28.3%	28.2%	28.2%
Drugs	14	23	37
	15.2%	29.5%	21.8%
Property	23	18	41
	25.0%	23.1%	24.1%
Vehicle	18	9	27
	19.6%	11.5%	15.9%
Other	11	6	17
	12.0%	7.7%	10.0%
Total	92	78	170
	100.0%	100.0%	100.0%
	Not Statistically Different		

Co-Occurring Disorder Measures

Table 4-7 provides the mean scores for five CAAPE-5 measures. The experimental group had higher average scores for all five variables. Further, the experimental group was also significantly higher for the Substance Abuse Score and Number of Drugs Severely Abused. Clearly, the experimental group had a greater substance abuse problem that could affect reentry and subsequent recidivism.

Overall, the random assignment of subjects produced statistically equivalent groups on most measures. The experimental group was slightly more educated (1 ½ grade level). None of the other demographic factors were significantly different. Prior criminal history is a highly important factor with respect to recidivism. However, the results showed that the two groups were statistically equivalent for all five criminal history variables. Of the five co-occurring disorder measures, two were significant. The experimental group had a significantly higher scores for substance abuse and the number of drugs severely abused. In theory, therefore, the experimental group might have a greater chance of recidivism to the extent that these two measures represent criminogenic factors.

Table 4-7. Mean Co-Occurring Disorder Measures

	Substance Abuse Score	**# of Drugs Abused**	**# of Drugs Severely Abused**	**Mental Health Score**	**# of Disorder Types**
Control	6.67	2.74	1.74	1.97	4.49
Experimental	8.35	3.12	2.46	2.06	4.58
Total	7.44	2.91	2.07	2.01	4.53
Significance	**Yes**	No	**Yes**	No	No

Chapter Five

Validating the Screening Instrument

Before this study can investigate the relationship between co-occurring disorders and the comparative criminal recidivism between the experimental and control groups, we must establish the scientific validity of the Comprehensive Addictions and Psychological Evaluation (CAAPE). As discussed above, the CAAPE is a screening instrument specifically designed to assess persons with co-occurring disorders (Hoffmann, 2000) within the same instrument. The CAAPE provides detailed indications of abuse for nine substances (alcohol, marijuana, cocaine, heroin, stimulants, sedatives, hallucinogens, inhalants, and a category for mixed substance abuse). The CAAPE also covers six Axis I and six Axis II DSM-IV conditions–the more prevalent mental health conditions likely to impact recovery from substance use disorders. The CAAPE has been applied to adjudicated adolescents in secure facilities (Abrantes, Hoffmann, and Anton, 2005) and in a comparative analysis of the relative prevalence of substance use disorders among prison inmates in the United Kingdom and the United States (Jones and Hoffman, 2006).

We are not aware of any rigorous, peer-reviewed validation studies of the CAAPE except for the following comparative analysis. In an evaluation of a day treatment program for co-occurring disorders, subjects were given the structured clinical interview for DSM-IV (SCID) and the CAAPE (Gallagher, Penn, Brooks, and Feldman, 2006). This study found that the concordance between the SCID and CAAPE on substance use disorders was very high (95%), but for mental health disorders, the concordance between SCID and CAAPE was much lower (40%, 8 out of 20 cases). Overall, the study concluded as follows. First, the CAAPE provides accurate and complete data for arriving at substance abuse diagnoses. Second, the CAAPE is less burdensome in terms of administration and interviewer training time. Third, the CAAPE needs further specification in the mental health modules in order to generate enough data to establish DSM diagnoses rather than just screen for them. However, the addition of a psychotic disorders module in a revised version addressed this shortcoming. Fourth, the attraction of the CAAPE is that it is relatively brief, and its format leaves less room for interpretation and clinical judgment, which might lead to more reliable diagnoses.

This chapter is a necessary extension of the research by Gallagher, Penn, Brooks, and Feldman (2006) and examines the CAAPE's construct validity among our sample of jail inmates. In common psychometric usage, validity is traditionally defined as "the degree to which a test measures what it claims, or purports, to be measuring" (Brown, 1996, p. 231). Traditionally, validity is subdivided into three categories: content, criterion, and construct (Brown 1996, pp. 231-249).

Content validity includes any assessment that focuses on the content of the measure and evaluates whether the measurement reflects a representative sample of whatever the concept should include. Criterion or concrete validity) is the extent to which a measure is related to an outcome of interest. Criterion validity can be specified as either concurrent or predictive. Concurrent validity refers to a comparison between the measure in question and a criterion variable assessed at the same time, while predictive validity is the degree of association between the scores and some other measure that the scores are designed to predict at a later point in time. Last, construct validity is defined as the empirical demonstration that a test or scale is actually capturing the construct it claims to be measuring.

The concept of validity is well established. In the behavioral and social sciences all three types of validity discussed above are now taken to represent different facets of a single unified form of construct validity (Messick, 1989). In social and behavioral research, a construct can be a psychometric attribute, proficiency, ability, or skill that happens in the human brain and is defined by established theories. A construct can also be a social phenomenon that arises in the social structure and affects people in empirically observable ways. Examples of social constructs could be strain, the culture of poverty, concentrated disadvantage, the subculture of violence and so on. In the present study, since the CAAPE purports to measure the co-morbidity of two related constructs–mental health disorders and substance abuse–we have adopted the unified view of validity and specify our exact inquiry as follows. If co-occurring disorders are related to criminal behavior as suggested by prior research, then there should be two empirical linkages. First, analogous to concurrent validity, each component of the CAAPE scores should be associated with the criminal history of the subjects prior to being enrolled in this experiment. Second, the CAAPE should also have predictive validity–the extent to which the scores are associated with the criminal recidivism of our subjects after they were released back into the community.

Variables

Independent Variables

CAAPE Drug Abuse

The CAAPE assesses drug abuse with four abuse levels: None, Mild, Moderate, and Severe which are scored from 0 to 3 for nine drugs (Alcohol, Marijuana, Cocaine, Stimulants, Sedatives, Heroin, Hallucinogens, Inhalants, and Mixed). The scores are summed to produce a *Total Drug Abuse Score* (range = 1-27). The minimum score is "1" because all cases must have a COD diagnosis to have been included in this experiment.

CAAPE Mental Health

The CAAPE screens nine mental health disorders (Major Depressive, Manic, Panic, Post Traumatic Stress, Anxiety, Obsessive/Compulsive, Psychosis, Anti-Social Personality, and Personality Disorder) and are scored absent / present. The items are then evaluated to produce an overall ***Mental Health Score*** (range = 1-3; Mild, Moderate, and Severe).

Dependent Variables

Prior Criminal History

The criminal history of the subjects is comprised of two measures. First, the count of arrests prior to the current offense which resulted in the incarceration of the subjects. Second, the count of the total number of charges for which the subject was convicted prior to the current jail commitment.

Reentry Recidivism

Recidivism status consists of any post-release infraction including technical violation, arrest for a new crime, or conviction for a new crime. The variables are thus count of arrests post-release or the count of convictions post-release.

Demographic Factors

In the following analyses we have used the following control variables: race (coded as other vs. White); number of years of school completed; marital status (single vs. married); and age in years at intake for the current incarceration.

Table 5-1 provides descriptive data for the variables. These data suggest that there is sufficient variation across the measures so that multi-variate analyses will not be hindered by a situation in which the cases are too homogenous to analyze effects–especially the predictive efficiency of the CAAPE measures. In terms of background factors, the sample is 49 percent White, has less than a high school education on average (11.39 years of schooling), is predominantly never married (82%), and ranges in age from 19.5 to 66.1 years old with an average of 33.16.

The data for the two prime CAAPE measures of interest here, the substance abuse and mental health scores, show that the subjects vary in the extent of their co-occurring disorders. The scores range from a low of one to a maximum of 21 on the substance abuse scale with a mean of 7.44, which indicates moderate substance abuse on average. The mental health scores range from a low of one (low disorders) to a maximum of 3 (severe disorders) and an average score of 2.01 which signifies moderate mental health problems.

The data for the five dependent variables also reflect sufficient variation so that analyses will not be hampered by limited scores reflective of minimum variation on the criterion measures. The number of prior arrests ranges from no prior crimes to a maximum of 65, with an average of 15.26 and a standard deviation of 13.519. Similarly, the number of criminal charges for which the sample was convicted previously ranges from no prior convictions to a maximum of 72 with a mean of 15.29 and a standard deviation of 14.4. The three post-release recidivism measures also show sufficient variation. Fifty three percent of the sample recidivated after release. The number of post-release arrests ranged from none to six with an average of .74. Those arrested were convicted of an average of 1.95 criminal charges with a maximum of 37.

Table 5-1. Descriptive Statistics

	N	Minimum	Maximum	Mean	Std. Dev.
Demographic					
Race Dummy	170	0	1	0.49	0.501
Highest Grade	170	4	17	11.35	2.076
Marital Dummy	170	0	1	0.18	0.387
Age at Intake	170	19.5	66.1	33.16	10.069
CAAPE					
Substance Abuse	170	1	21	7.44	4.847
Mental Health	170	1	3	2.01	0.754
Criminal History					
# of Prior Arrests	170	0	65	15.26	13.519
# of Prior Convictions	170	0	72	15.29	14.424
Post Recidivist Status	170	0	1	0.53	0.501
# of Post Arrests	170	0	6	0.78	1.243
# of Post Convictions	170	0	37	1.95	4.82

Analysis Strategy

The analyses below are a validation effort focusing on the construct validity of the CAAPE. This is a methodological inquiry and requires a particular type of statistical analysis.

First, four of the dependent variables are count measures. The appropriate statistical analysis for such data is a generalized linear model (Long, 1997; Cameron and Trivedi, 1998). We examined both Poisson regression and negative binomial models. As noted by Walters (2007), Poisson models are often the best fit for these data and this was the case here. The fifth dependent variable was a binary measure which necessitated the use of logistic regression.

Second, for all five dependent variables we tested mixed models which included both main effects and a continuous by continuous interaction effect of substance abuse score by mental health score. Because we are trying to validate the two dimensions of co-morbidity reflected in the

CAAPE measures, the interaction effect facilitates the investigation by examining the joint effects of these two prime measures (Allison, 1977; Allison, 1999). We are not hypothesizing that either of these measures act as mediators or moderators for one another (see Baron and Kenny, 1986). Instead, we are interested in the separate main effects of each of the CAAPE measures and whether they interact with one another to produce more than just additive effects when the measures co-vary.

Third, in all models we investigate the CAAPE summary scores after controlling for demographic factors (i.e., race, education, marital status, and age) which are generally associated with criminal behavior in their own right.

Findings

Prior Criminal Behavior

The Poisson regression results for the criminal history of the subjects prior to the current incarceration are reported in Tables 5-2 and 5-3. Table 5-2 provides the results concerning the count of prior arrests. All of the coefficients are significant with the exception of marital status. Whites have significantly fewer prior arrests; as education increases the count of arrests increases; and likewise, as age increases so too does the count of prior arrests. Marital status is unrelated to prior arrest count. Given these effects, it is important to control for these variables to investigate properly our prime interest in the CAAPE summary measures. The main effects of substance abuse and mental health scores are significant and positive, while the interaction effect is also significant and positive. This result is very interesting and comports with the concept of co-morbidity. The significant and positive interaction effect is referred to as a reinforcing or synergistic interaction (Afshartous and Preston, 2011). The effect of an increasing mental health score is more pronounced when the substance abuse score also increases and vice versa. Once the interaction effect is examined, we turn to the main effects of the two variables included in the interaction. These are known as conditional main effects (Afshartous and Preston, 2011). We see that the mental disorders coefficient (0.200) is much higher than substance abuse (0.044). This signifies that the count of arrests increases more for increases in the mental health score than it does for increases in the substance abuse scale score.

Table 5-2. Poisson Regression: Count of Prior Arrests

Parameter	*B*	S.E.	Wald Chi-Square	df	Sig.
Intercept	1.3	0.1782	53.231	1	**0.001**
Race: White	-0.161	0.0429	14.158	1	**0.001**
Marital: Ever Married	0.041	0.058	0.505	1	0.477
Highest Grade	0.025	0.0098	6.649	1	**0.010**
Age at Intake	0.021	0.0023	86.46	1	**0.001**
Substance Abuse	0.044	0.0115	14.348	1	**0.001**
Mental Health	0.200	0.0484	17.025	1	**0.001**
Substance Abuse MH Interaction	0.017	0.0054	10.357	1	**0.001**

Table 5-3 presents the Poisson regression results for the count of prior conviction charges. It is important to examine this variable because it captures the extent of prior criminality perhaps better than the arrest measure. That is, an offender could be arrested five times and be convicted of five charges, while another offender may also have five prior arrests but was convicted of ten or more charges. Clearly, these two criminal histories do not reflect the same degree of criminality. The Table 5.3 results are perhaps more definitive than those in Table 5-2. Table 5-3 indicates that only one demographic variable, age at intake, it significantly related to the total number of charges for which the offender had been convicted prior to his present incarceration. Age at intake can be a proxy for criminal career length and this result makes substantive sense. Like in Table 5.2, there is a significant reinforcing interaction effect of the mental health and substance abuse scores. And again, the conditional main effect of mental health is stronger (0.236) as opposed to substance abuse (0.057).

Analogous to the concept of criterion validity, the CAAPE identifies two dimensions of co-occurring disorders: a mental health disorders score and substance abuse score. At the time of the entry of the subjects into the county jail, these dimensions were significantly related to two different measures of prior criminal history.

Table 5-3. Poisson Regression: Count of Prior Convictions

Parameter	*B*	S.E.	Wald Chi-Square	df	Sig.
Intercept	0.874	0.1822	22.984	1	**0.000**
Race: White	0.082	0.0436	3.529	1	**0.060**
Marital: Ever Married	0.072	0.0574	1.579	1	0.209
Highest Grade	0.010	0.0099	0.002	1	0.966
Age at Intake	0.029	0.0022	163.426	1	**0.000**
Substance Abuse	0.057	0.0112	25.879	1	**0.000**
Mental Health	0.236	0.0489	23.32	1	**0.000**
Substance Abuse MH Interaction	0.010	0.005	4.067	1	**0.044**

Post-Release Recidivism

This research is also interested in the extent to which the CAAPE validly identifies the components of co-occurring disorders so that the scores can be used to predict or explain the criminal behavior of the subjects upon release back into society. The present subjects served on average about six months incarceration prior to release. Since co-occurring disorders are significant criminogenic factors, and since these disorders are likely a chronic condition, and since only focused, therapeutic intervention is likely to remediate the disorders, then higher scores on the mental disorders and substance abuse dimensions should be related to post-release recidivism–hence, the predictive validity of the CAAPE. We have three recidivism measures available. As above, we have the count of both arrests and conviction charges. But we also have a dichotomous measure of recidivism–Yes or No. Moreover, in the following analyses we can also control for the extent of prior criminality as a competing variable to the CAAPE scores. Prior criminal behavior is usually the strongest predictor of recidivism, so it will be instructive to see how well the CAAPE measures compete with this variable.

Table 5-4. Logistic Regression of Recidivism Status

Parameter	B	S.E.	Wald	df	Sig.	Exp(B)
Race: White	-0.325	0.349	0.864	1	0.353	0.723
Highest Grade	0.025	0.086	0.084	1	0.772	1.025
Marital: Ever Married	0.550	0.512	1.156	1	0.282	1.733
Age at Intake	-0.054	0.021	6.486	1	0.011	0.948
Prior Arrests	0.012	0.013	0.841	1	0.359	1.012
Substance Abuse	0.226	0.102	4.969	1	0.026	1.254
Mental Health	1.087	0.416	6.824	1	0.009	2.964
Substance Abuse MH Interaction	0.102	0.046	4.845	1	0.028	0.903
Constant	0.782	1.461	0.287	1	0.592	0.457

Table 5-4 provides the logistic regression results for recidivism status–whether the subject had any arrests or not after release into the community. The only demographic factor that is significant is age at intake. The older an inmate is, the less likely he is to be a recidivist. Interestingly, the extent of prior criminality is not a significant predictor of recidivism status. However, the CAAPE measures are significant as found previously. The mental health scores and substance abuse scores have a significant reinforcing interaction. Likewise, the conditional main effects are also significant and indicate that the strongest predictor of recidivism status is mental health score (1.087) as compared to substance abuse (0.226). Logistic regression also provides the odds associated with a given predictor. These odds confirm these effects as well. A high mental health score produces 2.964 greater likelihood of becoming a recidivist as compared to substance abuse for which the odds are 1.254.

Table 5-5. Poisson Regression: Count of Recidivism Arrests

Parameter	*B*	S.E.	Wald Chi-Square	df	Sig.
Intercept	-0.529	0.8475	0.39	1	0.532
Race: White	-0.314	0.1857	2.859	1	0.091
Marital: Ever Married	-0.394	0.2918	1.825	1	0.177
Highest Grade	-0.030	0.0502	0.368	1	0.544
Age at Intake	-0.043	0.0128	11.328	1	**0.001**
Prior Arrests	0.021	0.0058	12.736	1	**0.000**
Substance Abuse	0.140	0.0534	6.832	1	**0.009**
Mental Health	0.831	0.2451	11.501	1	**0.001**
Substance Abuse MH Interaction	0.061	0.0245	6.251	1	**0.012**

Table 5-5 reports the Poisson regression model for the count of arrests after release. These results are very similar to Table 5-4. Age at intake is significant and negatively associated with the number of arrests after release. Prior criminal history is significant and positively associated with the number of recidivist arrests. The measures of prime interest, the CAAPE scores, mirror the findings from all previous analyses. Mental health disorders and substance abuse show a reinforcing interaction such that high scores on each dimension is significantly associated with the count of arrests. Likewise, the contingent effects reveal that mental health disorders has a stronger effect (0.831) as compared to substance abuse (0.140).

The most interesting findings are contained in Table 5-6 concerning the extent of the charges for which the subject was convicted upon release into the community. First, all demographic factors are significant and in the expected direction: Whites have fewer charges; subjects that were ever married have fewer charges; the higher the education the fewer recidivism charges; the older a subject is the fewer the charges; and the higher the number of prior arrests the greater the number of post-release convictions. The findings for the CAAPE measures are identical to those reported above. The two dimensions of co-morbidity, mental health disorders and substance abuse show a significant reinforcing interaction. The conditional main effects indicate that the mental health disorders factor (1.387) is stronger than substance abuse (0.207).

Conclusion

The goal of this aspect of the study was to add to a growing body of research concerning the relationship between co-occurring disorders and criminal behavior by investigating the construct validity of the CAAPE. The results of rigorous multi-variate models indicated that the CAAPE appears to have construct validity because it captured two principal components of co-morbidity: mental health disorders and substance abuse. The findings with respect to five different criminal history measures were definitive.

First, the CAAPE measures were significant, mutually reinforcing factors of criminal behavior. Second, the mental disorders component was stronger than the effect of substance abuse. Third, the CAAPE measures remained significant after controlling for many other variables that are usually related to criminal behavior and often have very strong effects in their own right. Here, however, the CAAPE measures were stronger and had significant effects.

These results indicate that further research is warranted to provide additional validation data for the CAAPE. Such research should cross-validate the CAAPE with justice-involved persons with other co-occurring disorder screening instruments. It would also be advisable to investigate the comparative validity of the CAAPE with varying samples of offenders–those in jails and those in state prison serving longer sentences.

The results reported here nevertheless suggest a pressing need to assess offenders upon entry to correctional facilities and then again before release. The CAAPE measures were significantly related to prior criminal record and it is likely that co-morbidity was an important criminogenic factor. Moreover, because co-morbidity was also related to post release recidivism, it is also likely that co-morbidity represents a chronic condition which drives criminality even after incarceration ends if it is not properly treated. Clinicians would be wise to assess all inmates with tools such as the CAAPE so that co-occurring disorders can be identified and focused treatment undertaken. This is the case because both institutional adjustment and future recidivism upon community reentry seem clearly connected causally.

Table 5-6. Poisson Regression: Count of Recidivism Convictions

Parameter	*B*	S.E.	Wald Chi-Square	df	Sig.
Intercept	2.199	0.5397	16.601	1	**0.000**
Race: White	-0.423	0.1235	11.736	1	**0.001**
Marital: Ever Married	-1.051	0.1782	34.771	1	**0.000**
Highest Grade	-0.147	0.032	21.008	1	**0.000**
Age at Intake	-0.083	0.0089	86.3	1	**0.000**
Prior Arrests	0.02	0.0038	27.274	1	**0.000**
Substance Abuse	0.207	0.0386	28.703	1	**0.000**
Mental Health	1.387	0.1708	65.961	1	**0.000**
Substance Abuse MH Interaction	0.097	0.0171	32.109	1	**0.000**

CHAPTER SIX

RECIDIVISM: EXPERIMENTAL VS. CONTROL GROUPS

This chapter provides the findings from the analyses of the quantitative outcomes of the experimental COD treatment program. These results concern the various comparisons from the analysis of the recidivism outcome variables for the experimental and control groups. These analyses are further divided into two components: (1) descriptive tables; and (2) main effect, multivariate regression models. Chapter 7 focuses on the experimental group only so that we can examine the number, type, and timing of reentry services delivered and the extent to which these program variables were related to experimental group recidivism. Chapter 8 provides the findings from the process analysis in order to shed light on the possible reasons for experimental group recidivism.

Descriptive Analyses of Recidivism

In this research we measured recidivism in as many ways as possible given the specifics of the criminal history data available in Massachusetts. Through the measurement of multiple categorical and quantitative recidivism variables, we have provided for multiple opportunities to compare the recidivism of the experimental vs. control groups. In particular, we measured whether the recidivism was for a new offense as opposed to a technical violation. Thus, we had available the following nine measures of crime committed after reentry back into the community as of 31 January 2017:

- Any type of recidivism (encompassing the following three measures):
    - Arrested for a technical violation of parole;
    - Arrested for a new crime;
    - Arrested and convicted of one or more new charges;
- Number of arrests;
- Number of charges for which offender was subsequently convicted;

- Most serious offense type for arrest and/or conviction;
- Offense severity scale of new crime (measured from 0 - 7 based on crime code ranking; and
- Time in days between release from prison and date of recidivism.

Ultimately, therefore, the descriptive measures capture multiple dimensions of recidivism to determine whether the experimental group exhibited lower recidivism than did the control group.

Table 6-1 provides the overall recidivism results for the experimental and control groups. These data indicate that the experimental group had a higher percentage of recidivists (55.1%) as compared to the control group (51.1%).

Despite the provision of a variety of services to the experimental group, it would be expected that the experimental group would exhibit a significantly lower percentage of recidivists. Overall, therefore, the reentry services provided to adult offenders with co-occurring disorders was not successful.

Table 6-2 provides the results concerning the issue of recidivism across the two groups as measured by whether the recidivism was only a technical violation of probation or parole as opposed to a new crime. These data indicate that among the 90 recidivists shown in Table 6-2, the experimental group did have a higher percentage of administrative violations. But the result was not statistically significant.

Table 6-3 indicates that the experimental group had a slightly lower percentage (72.1) of recidivists who were arrested for a new crime as compared to the control group (76.6%). Likewise, Table 6-4 shows that the experimental group had a slightly lower percentage (37.2%) who had been convicted of new charges as compared to the control group (38.3%). In both these situations, however, the differences were slight and were not significant.

Tables 6-1 through 6-4 only address the status of recidivist and do not address the character, extent, or timing of the recidivism. These findings are shown in Tables 6.5 and 6.6.

Table 6-1. Overall Recidivism

Recidivism		Control	Experimental	Total
No	Count	45	35	80
	%	48.9%	44.9%	47.1%
Yes	Count	47	43	90
	%	51.1%	55.1%	52.9%
Total	Count	92	78	170
	%	100.0%	100.0%	100.0%
	Not Statistically Different			

Table 6-2. Technical Recidivism

Technical		Control	Experimental	Total
No	Count	24	17	41
	%	51.1%	39.5%	45.6%
Yes	Count	23	26	49
	%	48.9%	60.5%	54.4%
Total	Count	47	43	90
	%	100.0%	100.0%	100.0%
	Not Statistically Different			

Table 6-3. Arrest Recidivism

Arrest		Control	Experimental	Total
No	Count	11	12	23
	%	23.40%	27.90%	25.60%
Yes	Count	36	31	67
	%	76.60%	72.10%	74.40%
Total	Count	47	43	90
	%	100.00%	100.00%	100.00%
	Not Statistically Different			

Table 6-4. Conviction Recidivism

Conviction		Control	Experimental	Total
No	Count	29	27	56
	%	61.7%	62.8%	62.2%
Yes	Count	18	16	34
	%	38.3%	37.2%	37.8%
Total	Count	47	43	90
	%	100.0%	100.0%	100.0%
	Not Statistically Different			

Table 6-5 provides the recidivism in the two groups with respect to the most serious offense with which the recidivist had been charged. Although we have found that the status of recidivism as shown in Tables 6.1 through 6.4 was equivalent in the two groups, we needed to investigate the character of the recidivism. Table 6.5 indicates that the experimental group actually had the greater severity of offense type. That is, the experimental group's percentage for violence (18.6% vs. 14.9%), for drug offenses (16.3% vs. 8.5%) and for property crimes (16.3% vs. 8.5%) was higher than was the case for the control group. Alternatively, the control group was more likely to have committed a vehicular offense (19.1% vs. 11.6%) and the residual "other" category of less serious crimes (27.7% vs. 14.-%). As before however, none of these differences were statistically significant.

Table 6-6 provides the results for the four quantitative variables which provide other important comparisons across the two groups. First, the experimental group had a higher offense scale score for recidivism. Second, however, the control group had a higher average number of arrests and convictions. Third, the experimental group did, on average, recidivate more quickly by a factor of 11 days. Ultimately, as we have seen previously concerning the categorical variables, none of these quantitative differences reached statistical significance.

The findings for the descriptive measures were very definitive. Across five categorical variables and four quantitative variables of recidivism, none of the comparisons revealed significant findings. For all measures, the experimental and control groups had statistically equivalent recidivism data. These findings indicate that the program failed to reduce recidivism for subjects in the experimental group despite having received reentry services as opposed to the control group who did not receive any community-based services at all.

Table 6-5. Recidivism Offense Type

Offense		**Control**	**Experimental**	**Total**
Violence	Count	7	8	15
	%	14.9%	18.6%	16.7%
Drugs	Count	4	7	11
	%	8.5%	16.3%	12.2%
Property	Count	4	7	11
	%	8.5%	16.3%	12.2%
Vehicle	Count	9	5	14
	%	19.1%	11.6%	15.6%
Other	Count	13	6	19
	%	27.7%	14.0%	21.1%
Violation	Count	10	10	20
	%	21.3%	23.3%	22.2%
Total	Count	47	43	90
	%	100.0%	100.0%	100.0%
	Not Statistically Different			

Table 6-6. Quantitative Recidivism Measures

	# of Post Arrests	**# of Post Convictions**	**Post Offense Scale**	**Time to Recidivism**
Control	1.49	3.77	2.09	187.19
Experimental	1.47	3.60	2.15	175.21
Total	1.48	3.69	2.12	181.47
Significance	No	No	No	No

Multi-variate Analyses of Recidivism

While essential to capture the distributional parameters of the recidivism dependent variable, and offer simple bivariate significance tests, descriptive analyses do not permit examination of the dependent variable while controlling for other predictor variables that could be influencing the recidivism criterion measures. This can only be accomplished with multivariate models. In the present case, we have both dichotomous and quantitative measures of recidivism. Logistic Regression is a special type of multiple regression when the dependent variable is a binary variable and the researcher wants to examine the effects of a set of explanatory variables (which can be discrete and/or continuous). An important distinction is that in linear regression, the expected values of the response variable are estimated based on combination of values taken by the predictors, while in logistic regression it is the probability or odds of the response taking a particular value that is predicted based on combination of values taken by the predictors. In the case where the dependent variable is quantitative, we have used the following analyses. Both the arrest and conviction measures are count variables. For these, the appropriate analysis technique is Poisson regression (or negative binomial regression) depending on distributional issues. For the recidivism scale and time to failure, Ordinary Least Squares regression is the appropriate technique.

Prediction of Types of Recidivist Status

The logistic regression models for the four dichotomous recidivism measures are reported in Tables 6-7 to 6-10. The main goal of these models was to determine whether the program variable (experimental vs. control) had a significant effect on the alternate ways of measuring recidivism status. The models also estimate the effects of three other blocks of variables (demographic, criminal history, and co-occurring disorder scores) as covariates. The results for all four models are definitive–the program did not result in lower recidivism for the experimental group. By virtue of the sign of the coefficient for the program variable, the experimental group was more likely to be an overall recidivist and a technical violator, while the control group was more likely to be arrested or convicted. But, none of these coefficients were significant.

These four models did show some significant coefficients which are important and should be considered for reentry programs.

First, age-at-release was a significant negative predictor of overall recidivism status. This suggests perhaps that the older an inmate gets, the less likely to recidivate upon reentry.

Second, time served was a significant negative predictor of recidivism status thus suggesting that the longer the current period of incarceration the less likely the inmate behaves in a manner which would send him back to prison.

Third, age-at-release was also a significant predictor of the arrest version of recidivism. This substantiates the age effect reported above.

Last, the results for conviction status confirm the previous findings concerning less severe recidivism and also show a familiar criminogenic effect. That is, age-at-release and time served were found to be significant negative predictors of conviction. Further, however, the results also showed that as the number of prior convictions increase, the more likely that the subject will be convicted of multiple charges. These are familiar criminological effects.

Prediction of Quantitative Recidivism Measures

The analyses for the four quantitative measures of recidivism are given in Tables 6-11 to 6-14. Like the binary variables reported above, the quantitative models were also definitive. The program did not produce diminished recidivism when measured quantitatively. The program variable was not significant in any of the four analyses. Although not significant, the coefficients do indicate some interesting effects. The experimental group was more likely to accumulate a higher number of arrests, but a fewer number of convictions. Also, the experimental group had a lower recidivism offense scale score, but it also had a faster time to failure.

The quantitative analyses showed a few coefficients of interest.

First, the number of prior convictions had a significant, positive coefficient on the count of recidivism arrests.

Second, there were multiple significant coefficients for the model analyzing the count of conviction charges. Two demographic predictors, marital status and years of school completed had significant, negative effects on convictions. In addition, three substance abuse variables, substance abuse score, number of drugs abused, and number of drugs severely abused, had significant, positive effects on the number of convictions.

Third, the number of drugs severely abused also had a significant, positive effect on the severity of the recidivism offense. Last, when compared to whites, all other race/ethnic categories had a significantly shorter time for recidivism to occur.

The multi-variate models of binary and quantitative recidivism measures indicated that only familiar criminological and demographic variables were significantly related to recidivism, while program membership was not.

Summary

In this chapter we reported the results for the comparison of the recidivism between the experimental and control groups. Given that a variety of reentry services were provided to the experimental group, it would certainly be expected that the experimental group would exhibit a significantly lower percentage of recidivists, regardless of the particular way in which recidivism was measured. We analyzed bi-variate cross-tabulations across four measures of recidivism. We also analyzed the type of recidivism offense. We compared the mean number of recidivism offenses.

The findings for the descriptive analyses were unequivocal. Across five categorical variables and four quantitative variables of recidivism, none of the comparisons revealed significant findings. For all measures, the experimental and control groups had statistically equivalent recidivism data. These findings indicate that the program failed to reduce recidivism for subjects in the experimental group despite having received reentry services as opposed to the control group who did not receive any community-based services at all.

It is unwise to develop strong conclusions using only basic descriptive analyses. While such descriptive analyses are essential to capture the distributional parameters of the recidivism dependent variable, descriptive analyses do not permit examination of the dependent variable while controlling for other predictor variables that could be influencing the recidivism criterion measures. This can only be accomplished with multivariate models. In the present case, we had both dichotomous and quantitative measures of recidivism. Thus, we analyzed the data using rigorous modeling techniques such as logistic regression, Poisson regression, and ordinary least squares regression.

We conducted logistic regression models for the four dichotomous recidivism measures to determine whether the program variable (experimental vs. control) had a significant effect on the alternate measures of recidivism status. The models also included the effects of three other blocks of variables (demographic, criminal history, and co-occurring disorder scores) as covariates. The results for all four models were unequivocal–the program did not result in lower recidivism for the experimental group. By virtue of the sign of the coefficient for the program variable, the experimental group was more likely to be an overall recidivist and a technical violator, while the control group was more likely to be arrested or convicted. But, none of these coefficients were significant.

The analyses for the four quantitative measures of recidivism, like the binary variables reported above, were also unequivocal. The program did not produce diminished recidivism when measured quantitatively. The program variable was not significant in any of the four analyses. Although not significant, the coefficients do indicate some interesting effects. The experimental group was more likely to accumulate a higher number of arrests, but a fewer number of convictions. Also, the experimental group had a lower recidivism offense scale score, but it also had a faster time to failure.

Further, the multivariate models concerning both the binary recidivism status variables and the quantitative recidivism counts indicated that only familiar criminological and demographic variables were significantly related to recidivism, while program membership was not.

All of these rigorous statistical techniques failed to uncover any evidence that the reentry services provided to the experimental group made any difference whatsoever in terms of recidivism.

Table 6-7. Logistic Regression of Overall Recidivist Status

	B	S.E.	Wald	Sig.	Exp(B)
PROGRAM					
Experimental Group	0.074	0.348	0.045	0.832	1.077
DEMOGRAPHIC					
Race Dummy	-0.299	0.367	0.661	0.416	0.742
Marital Dummy	0.509	0.52	0.955	0.328	1.663
Highest Grade	0.028	0.092	0.094	0.759	1.029
CRIMINAL HISTORY					
Age at Release	-0.057	0.024	5.792	**0.016**	0.945
Time Served	-0.034	0.04	0.719	0.396	0.967
Number of Prior Arrests	-0.005	0.016	0.084	0.773	0.995
Number of Prior Convictions	0.029	0.017	3.056	0.08	1.03
Commitment Offense Scale	0.033	0.08	0.168	0.682	1.033
CO-OCCURRING DISORDERS					
Substance Abuse Score	0.162	0.299	0.292	0.589	1.175
Number of Drugs Abused	-0.166	0.469	0.126	0.723	0.847
Number of Drugs Severely Abused	-0.31	0.487	0.406	0.524	0.733
Mental Health Score	0.081	0.555	0.021	0.884	1.084
Number of Disorder Types	0.12	0.258	0.216	0.642	1.127
Constant	0.61	1.56	0.153	0.696	1.84

Table 6-8. Logistic Regression of Technical Violation Status

	B	S.E.	Wald	Sig.	Exp(B)
PROGRAM					
Experimental Group	0.29	0.391	0.55	0.458	1.337
DEMOGRAPHIC					
Race Dummy	-0.736	0.415	3.148	0.076	0.479
Marital Dummy	0.074	0.588	0.016	0.9	1.076
Highest Grade	-0.112	0.103	1.18	0.277	0.894
CRIMINAL HISTORY					
Age at Release	-0.022	0.026	0.702	0.402	0.979
Time Served	-0.166	0.059	7.827	**0.005**	0.847
Prior Arrests	-0.006	0.018	0.113	0.737	0.994
Prior Convictions	0.006	0.019	0.098	0.754	1.006
Commitment Offense Scale	0.146	0.09	2.638	0.104	1.157
CO-OCCURRING DISORDERS					
Substance Abuse Score	0.249	0.317	0.614	0.433	1.282
Number of Drugs Abused	-0.397	0.518	0.587	0.443	0.673
Number of Drugs Severely Abused	-0.239	0.501	0.227	0.634	0.787
Mental Health Score	-0.403	0.591	0.465	0.495	0.668
Number of Disorder Types	0.3	0.271	1.224	0.269	1.35
Constant	0.583	1.733	0.113	0.737	1.791

Table 6-9. Logistic Regression of Arrest Status

	B	S.E.	Wald	Sig.	Exp(B)
PROGRAM					
Experimental Group	-0.041	0.352	0.014	0.907	0.96
DEMOGRAPHIC					
Race Dummy	-0.309	0.369	0.702	0.402	0.734
Marital Dummy	0.621	0.531	1.371	0.242	1.862
Highest Grade	-0.005	9.70E-02	0.002	0.96	0.995
CRIMINAL HISTORY					
Age at Release	-0.06	0.025	5.629	**0.018**	0.942
Time Served	0.002	0.04	0.004	0.951	1.002
Prior Arrests	0.005	0.016	0.1	0.752	1.005
Prior Convictions	0.027	0.016	2.873	0.09	1.028
Commitment Offense Scale	0.009	0.082	0.013	0.909	1.009
CO-OCCURRING DISORDERS					
Substance Abuse Score	-0.143	0.301	0.225	0.635	0.867
Number of Drugs Abused	0.13	0.468	0.077	0.781	1.139
Number of Drugs Severely Abused	0.328	0.494	0.441	0.507	1.388
Mental Health Score	0.569	0.569	1.001	0.317	1.767
Number of Disorder Types	-0.256	0.269	0.903	0.342	0.774
Constant	1.117	1.611	0.48	0.488	3.055

Table 6-10. Logistic Regression of Conviction Status

	B	S.E.	Wald	Sig.	Exp(B)
PROGRAM					
Experimental Group	-0.191	0.472	0.164	0.685	0.826
DEMOGRAPHIC					
Race Dummy	-1.148	0.51	5.069	0.024	0.317
Marital Dummy	1.523	0.679	5.023	0.025	4.584
Highest Grade	-0.297	0.135	4.856	0.028	0.743
CRIMINAL HISTORY					
Age at Release	-0.068	0.033	4.233	**0.041**	0.934
Time Served	-0.181	0.064	7.9	**0.005**	0.834
Prior Arrests	-0.002	0.02	0.007	0.931	0.998
Prior Convictions	0.059	0.022	7.393	**0.007**	1.06
Commitment Offense Scale	0.131	0.11	1.423	0.233	1.14
CO-OCCURRING DISORDERS					
Substance Abuse Score	-0.691	0.546	1.599	0.206	0.501
Number of Drugs Abused	0.533	0.769	0.48	0.488	1.704
Number of Drugs Severely Abused	1.662	0.953	3.043	0.081	5.272
Mental Health Score	0.096	0.708	0.018	0.892	1.101
Number of Disorder Types	0.033	0.328	0.01	0.921	1.034
Constant	3.419	2.226	2.358	0.125	30.525

Table 6-11. Poisson Regression of Arrest Count

	B	Std. Error	Chi-Square	Sig.
Intercept	0.903	0.9298	0.942	0.332
PROGRAM				
Experimental group	0.133	0.1904	0.485	0.486
DEMOGRAPHIC				
Race Dummy	0.168	0.192	0.768	0.381
Marital Dummy	-0.152	0.2917	0.27	0.603
Highest Grade	-0.042	0.0548	0.589	0.443
CRIMINAL HISTORY				
Age at Release	-0.021	0.0139	2.378	0.123
Time Served	0.034	0.021	2.629	0.105
Prior Arrests	0.01	0.0083	1.55	0.213
Prior Convictions	0.015	0.0073	4.384	**0.036**
Commitment Offense Scale	0.001	0.0444	0.001	0.973
CO-OCCURRING DISORDERS				
Substance Abuse Score	-0.208	0.194	1.149	0.284
Number of Drugs Abused	0.077	0.2968	0.067	0.796
Number of Drugs Severely Abused	0.581	0.3204	3.288	0.07
Mental Health Score	0.109	0.2838	0.146	0.702
Number of Disorder Types	-0.036	0.1317	0.074	0.786

Table 6-12. Poisson Regression of Conviction Count

	B	Std. Error	Chi-Square	Sig.
Intercept	2.416	0.6586	13.452	0.001
Experimental Group	-0.086	0.1259	0.469	0.494
DEMOGRAPHIC				
Race Dummy	0.199	0.1293	2.377	0.123
Marital Dummy	-0.586	0.1794	10.679	**0.001**
Highest Grade	-0.112	0.0365	9.38	**0.002**
CRIMINAL HISTORY				
Age at Release	-0.043	0.0093	20.869	**0.001**
Time Served	-0.087	0.013	44.897	**0.001**
Prior Arrests	0.009	0.0059	2.626	0.105
Prior Convictions	0.015	0.0049	10.003	**0.002**
Commitment Offense Scale	0.026	0.0322	0.632	0.427
CO-OCCURRING DISORDERS				
Substance Abuse Score	0.503	0.144	12.206	**0.001**
Number of Drugs Abused	0.486	0.2084	5.429	**0.02**
Number of Drugs Severely Abused	1.01	0.2464	16.785	**0.001**
Mental Health Score	0.113	0.182	0.383	0.536
Number of Disorder Types	0.144	0.0812	3.139	0.076

Table 6-13. OLS Regression of Recidivism Scale

	B	Std. Error	Standard. Beta	t	Sig.
Constant	3.119	0.774		4.031	0.001
PROGRAM					
Experimental Group	-0.155	0.173	-0.101	-0.9	0.371
DEMOGRAPHIC					
Race Dummy	-0.187	0.173	-0.121	-1.077	0.285
Marital Dummy	0.48	0.269	0.232	1.785	0.078
Highest Grade	-0.071	0.045	-0.174	-1.569	0.121
CRIMINAL HISTORY					
Age at Release	-0.005	0.012	-0.059	-0.411	0.682
Time Served	0.001	0.02	0.005	0.043	0.966
Prior Arrests	0.003	0.008	0.062	0.435	0.665
Prior Convictions	0.012	0.007	0.238	1.644	0.104
Commitment Offense Scale	0.009	0.038	0.026	0.238	0.812
CO-OCCURRING DISORDERS					
Substance Abuse Score	-0.265	0.14	-1.614	-1.891	0.062
Number of Drugs Abused	0.267	0.228	0.606	1.17	0.246
Number of Drugs Severely Abused	0.596	0.221	1.243	2.697	**0.009**
Mental Health Score	0.142	0.253	0.132	0.561	0.576
Number of Disorder Types	-0.126	0.118	-0.256	-1.068	0.289

Table 6-14. OLS Regression of Time to Failure (Days)

	B	Std. Error	Std. Beta	t	Sig.
Constant	151.876	108.15		1.404	0.164
PROGRAM					
Experimental Group	-16.857	24.159	-0.081	-0.698	0.487
DEMOGRAPHIC					
Race Dummy	51.744	24.218	0.247	2.137	**0.036**
Marital Dummy	-37.596	37.598	-0.134	-1	0.321
Highest Grade	4.312	6.289	0.078	0.686	0.495
CRIMINAL HISTORY					
Age at Release	0.313	1.612	0.029	0.194	0.846
Time Served	0.655	2.833	0.027	0.231	0.818
Prior Arrests	0.809	1.087	0.109	0.744	0.459
Prior Convictions	0.1	1.034	0.014	0.097	0.923
Commitment Offense Scale	-9.55	5.33	-0.202	-1.792	0.077
CO-OCCURRING DISORDERS					
Substance Abuse Score	-10.791	19.594	-0.485	-0.551	0.583
Number of Drugs Abused	35.006	31.839	0.588	1.099	0.275
Number of Drugs Severely Abused	0.581	30.867	0.009	0.019	0.985
Mental Health Score	2.505	35.342	0.017	0.071	0.944
Number of Disorder Types	-9.203	16.503	-0.138	-0.558	0.57

CHAPTER SEVEN

EXPERIMENTAL GROUP FAILURE

Experimental Group Analyses

None of the analyses reported in Chapter Six indicated that the experimental COD reentry program made any difference with respect to multiple measures of recidivism. This was highly unexpected. It is necessary at this juncture, therefore, to focus on the experimental group itself and examine descriptive data and multi-variate models which compare the experimental group recidivists to the experimental group non-recidivists. These analyses may provide insight concerning possible reasons why more than 50 percent of the experimental group recidivated despite receiving reentry services as compared to the control group who received no such services.

Descriptive Analyses

Table 7-1 provides LS/CMI Section 1 scores. The LS/CMI was administered as part of the discharge process just before reentry. The LS/CMI was implemented to inform the discharge plan and thus form a bridge to services needed upon reentry. Table 7.1 indicates that the overall score and the eight subscales were higher for the experimental group recidivists, thus indicating a clinical diagnosis of greater problems than the experimental group subjects that did not recidivate. Further, the total score, Family/Marital issues, and Pro Crime Attitude subscales were significantly higher for the recidivists. It would be expected, therefore, that these clinical indicators would lead to highly focused discharge planning so that reentry services could be tailored to these high-risk cases and focused on these risk factors. Available information would suggest that this did not happen. More discussion of this issue follows in Chapter Eight.

Table 7-1. Mean LS/CMI Scores for Experimental Group

Recidivist Status	LS/CMI Total	LS/CMI Criminal History	LS/CMI Education & Employment	LS/CMI Family & Marital	LS/CMI Leisure & Recreation
No	23.34	5.77	4.91	1.03	1.74
Yes	26.58	6.26	5.53	1.56	1.81
Total	25.13	6.04	5.26	1.32	1.78
Significance	**Yes**	No	No	**Yes**	No

Recidivist Status	LS/CMI Companions	LS/CMI Alcohol & Drugs	LS/CMI Pro-Crime Attitude	LS/CMI Anti-Social Pattern
No	2.66	5.11	0.71	1.4
Yes	2.84	5.42	1.37	1.79
Total	2.76	5.28	1.08	1.62
Significance	No	No	**Yes**	No

Table 7-2 shows very clearly that the recidivist subset had greater risk of recidivism for all the criminal history factors. Recidivists had higher prior arrests, had longer time served, and were younger. Most important, the experimental recidivists had a significantly higher number of prior convictions, which we have seen in the previous analyses was definitively related to recidivism for all cases, both experimental and control. Similarly, Table 7-3 indicates that Experimental recidivists had higher CAAPE scores for all five measures reflective of co-occurring disorders but these differences were not significant.

Table 7-2. Mean Criminal History Scores for Experimental Group

Recidivist Status		Prior Arrests	Prior Convictions	Time Served	Age at Release
No	Mean	12.11	10.83	3.96	34.06
	n = 35				
Yes	Mean	16.21	18.53	4.59	31.72
	n = 43				
Total	Mean	14.37	15.08	4.31	32.77
	n = 78				
Significance		No	**Yes**	No	No

Table 7-3. Mean Co-Occurring Disorder Scores

Recidivist Status		Substance Abuse Score	Number of Drugs Abused	Number of Drugs Severely Abused	MH Score	Number of Disorder Types
No	Mean	7.77	2.94	2.26	2.03	4.43
	n = 35					
Yes	Mean	8.81	3.26	2.63	2.09	4.7
	n = 43					
Total	Mean	8.35	3.12	2.46	2.06	4.58
	n = 78					
Significance		No	No	No	No	No

Tables 7-4 and 7-5 provide mean scores for the nine drugs of abuse scales (range = 0-3) and the nine mental health disorders (0,1) from the CAAPE instrument. Seventeen of the 18 mean scores were not significantly different between the recidivists and non-recidivists in the experimental group. Only in the case of cocaine was the difference significant and this coefficient indicated that the experimental group had a significantly higher mean level of involvement with cocaine.

Table 7-6 exhibits the case manager data for the experimental group. Although case manager “A” had a much higher percentage of cases (62.5%) who became recidivists than either case manager “B” (51.6%) or “C” (54.8%), the differences were not statistically significant.

The reentry services data are shown in Tables 7-7 and 7-8. These results are also unremarkable. Table 7-7 shows that the experimental group recidivists, when compared to the non-recidivists, do not have a significantly different distribution of the number of reentry goals. Likewise, the mean scores shown in Table 7-8 indicate that there are no significant differences in the average number of goals targeted, number of goals achieved, or the percentage of goals achieved.

Table 7-4. Mean CAAPE Drugs of Abuse Scores

Recidivist Status		Alcohol	Marijuana	Cocaine	Stimulants	Sedatives	Heroin	Hallucinogens	Inhalants	Other
No	**Mean n = 35**	2.17	1.54	**1.17**	0.57	0.66	1.29	0.37	0	0
Yes	**Mean n = 43**	2.21	1.98	**1.81**	0.33	0.63	1.58	0.21	0	0.07
Total	**Mean n = 78**	2.19	1.78	**1.53**	0.44	0.64	1.45	0.28	0	0.04
Significance		No	No	**Yes**	No	No	No	No	No	No

Table 7-5. Mean CAAPE Mental Health Disorder Scores

Recidivist Status		Major Depressive	Manic Disorder	Panic Disorder	PTSD	Anxiety Disorder	Obsessive Compulsive	Psychosis	Anti-Social Personality	Personality Disorder
No	Mean n = 35	0.4	0.17	0.2	0.37	0.83	0.66	0.17	0.69	0.94
Yes	Mean n = 43	0.3	0.09	0.16	0.49	0.88	0.81	0.12	0.86	0.98
Total	Mean n = 78	0.35	0.13	0.18	0.44	0.86	0.74	0.14	0.78	0.96
Significance		No	No	No	No	No	No	No	No	No

Table 7-6. Case Manager Assignments

Recidivist		Case Manager			Total
		A	B	C	
No	Count	6	15	14	35
	%	37.5	48.4	45.2	44.9
Yes	Count	10	16	17	43
	%	62.5	51.6	54.8	55.1
Total	Count	16	31	31	78
	%	100	100	100	100
		Not Significantly Different			

Multi-variate Models

The descriptive data shown above identify a few interesting differences between the recidivists and non-recidivists in the experimental group. Thus, it is worthwhile to use multivariate models to try to uncover variables that could explain the factors that lead to recidivism. These models are reported in Tables 7-9 to 7-13.

Table 7-9 shows a Poisson regression of the number of charges for which the recidivist was convicted after reentering the community. The total LS/CMI score across Section 1 was a significant predictor of convictions. The higher the total score the more convictions that occurred. Likewise, Table 7.10 shows a Poisson regression model using the eight subscales of Section 1. It is highly important that all of these coefficients were significant predictors of the count of convictions. The criminal history, education/employment, family/marital, pro-crime attitudes, and anti-social patterns had significant, positive effects on convictions. These coefficients suggest that the experimental group subjects who had high scores on these five subscales posed significantly increased risk of recidivism. The reentry program did not address these client issues sufficiently to prevent the recidivism that would be a natural consequence of these risk factors.

In addition to these LS/CMI effects, we also found significant co-occurring disorder effects. In Table 7-11we see that the total mental health score of the CAAPE had a significant and positive effect on convictions. Tables 7-12 and 7-13 examine specific factors contained in the overall substance abuse score and the mental health score. Table 7-12 indicates that subjects with a marijuana abuse profile had a significant and positive effect on convictions. However, alcohol and stimulant abusers had significant negative effects on convictions.

Table 7-13 presents very important findings because five of the nine disorder types had significant effects on recidivism–some were positive and some were negative. There were 3 CAAPE mental disorders that had significant and positive consequences for recidivism: PTSD, obsessive/compulsive, and anti-social personality. Experimental group subjects with these disorders accumulated a greater extent of post-release recidivism. Alternatively, there were two CAAPE disorders, major depressive and manic, that were significantly associated with a lower count of post-release convictions.

These multivariate results across the LS/CMI and CAAPE scores are important to corrections administrators, clinicians, and community reentry service organizations. These factors represent serious underlying disorders that must be remediated in order to reduce the risk of recidivism.

Table 7-7. Number of Service Goals

Service Goals		Recidivist Status		Total
		No	Yes	
0	Count	2	7	9
	%	5.7	16.3	11.5
1	Count	9	10	19
	%	25.7	23.3	24.4
2	Count	10	16	26
	%	28.6	37.2	33.3
3	Count	8	7	15
	%	22.9	16.3	19.2
4	Count	2	2	4
	%	5.7	4.7	5.1
5	Count	4	1	5
	%	11.4	2.3	6.4
Total	Count	35	43	78
	%	100	100	100
		Not Significantly Different		

Table 7-8. Mean Number of Goals, Goals Achieved, and Percent Achieved

Recidivist		# of Goals	# of Goals Achieved	% of Goals Achieved
No	Mean n = 35	2.31	1.43	0.49
Yes	Mean n = 43	1.77	0.95	0.43
Total	Mean n = 78	2.01	1.17	0.46
Significance		No	No	No

Table 7-9. Poisson Regression of Convictions and LS/CMI Score for Experimental Group

	B	Standard Error	Wald Chi-Square	Sig.
Intercept	-2.152	0.4394	23.997	0.001
LS/CMI Total	0.106	0.0152	48.515	**0.001**

Table 7-10. Poisson Regression of Convictions and LS/CMI Subscales for Experimental Group

	B	Standard Error	Wald Chi-Square	Sig.
Intercept	-1.921	0.6171	9.689	**0.002**
LS/CMI				
Criminal History	0.302	0.0854	12.518	**0.001**
Education/Employment	0.324	0.0568	32.505	**0.001**
Family/Marital	0.253	0.0896	7.971	**0.005**
Leisure/Recreation	-0.467	0.2359	3.922	**0.048**
Companions	0.138	0.0668	4.252	**0.039**
Alcohol/Drugs	-0.106	0.0528	4.01	**0.045**
Pro Crime Attitude	0.307	0.0908	11.451	**0.001**
Anti-Social Pattern	0.576	0.1472	15.341	**0.001**

Table 7-11. Poisson Regression of Convictions on CAAPE Scores for Experimental Group

	B	Standard Error	Wald Chi-Square	Sig.
Intercept	-0.118	0.3385	0.121	0.728
Substance Abuse Score	-0.286	0.2128	1.809	0.179
# of Drugs Abused	0.372	0.2894	1.648	0.199
# of Drugs Severely Abused	0.307	0.3798	0.652	0.419
MH Score	0.733	0.2634	7.745	**0.005**
Number of Disorder Types	-0.078	0.1216	0.415	0.519

Table 7-12. Poisson Regression of Convictions on CAAPE Drug Scores for Experimental Group

	B	Standard Error	Wald Chi-Square	Sig.
Intercept	0.892	0.1856	23.093	0.001
Alcohol	-0.395	0.0689	32.954	**0.001**
Marijuana	0.315	0.0768	16.812	**0.001**
Cocaine	0.061	0.0615	0.999	0.318
Stimulants	-0.346	0.1598	4.676	**0.031**
Sedatives	-0.07	0.0947	0.543	0.461
Heroin	0.036	0.0623	0.341	0.559
Hallucinogens	-0.313	0.2353	1.773	0.183
Inhalants	n.a.	n.a.	n.a.	n.a.
Other	0.025	0.2515	0.01	0.921

Table 7-13. Poisson Regression of Convictions on CAAPE Disorders for Experimental Group

	B	Standard Error	Wald Chi-Square	Sig.
Intercept	-2.825	1.105	6.538	**0.011**
Major Depressive	-0.875	0.211	17.18	**0.001**
Manic Disorder	-0.914	0.4108	4.947	**0.026**
Panic Disorder	-0.295	0.2305	1.638	0.201
PTSD	0.902	0.2019	19.963	**0.001**
Anxiety Disorder	-0.182	0.305	0.358	0.55
Obsessive / Compulsive	0.695	0.2997	5.375	**0.02**
Psychosis	0.377	0.2118	3.174	0.075
Anti -Social Personality	1.665	0.3321	25.15	**0.001**
Personality Disorder	1.484	1.0144	2.139	0.144

Summary of Experimental Group Analyses

Because none of the group comparison analyses indicated that the program made a significant difference with respect to multiple measures of recidivism, we then focused on the experimental group itself and examined descriptive data and multivariate models comparing the experimental group recidivists to the experimental group non-recidivists. These analyses identified possible reasons why more than 50 percent of the experimental group recidivated.

The descriptive data indicated that the overall LS/CMI score and the eight subscales were higher for the experimental group recidivists thus indicating a clinical diagnosis of greater problems than the experimental group subjects who did not recidivate. Further, the overall score, family/marital subscale and Pro Crime Attitude subscale were significantly higher for the recidivists. Likewise, the descriptive data showed very clearly that the recidivist subset had greater risk of recidivism for all the prior criminal history risk factors. Recidivists had higher prior arrests, had longer time served, and were younger. Most important, the experimental recidivists had a significantly higher number of prior convictions, which we have seen in previous analyses was definitively related to recidivism in this evaluation for all cases. The experimental recidivists had higher CAAPE scores for all five measures reflective of co-occurring disorders although these differences were not significant. However, only one of the CAAPE drugs of abuse, cocaine, showed a significant difference and this coefficient indicated that the experimental group had a significantly higher mean level of involvement with cocaine prior to the current incarceration.

The multivariate models of recidivism for the experimental group analyses did reveal some important results. The total LS/CMI score across Section 1 was a significant predictor of convictions. The higher the total score the more convictions that occurred. Likewise, for the eight subscales of the LS/CMI Section 1, four of these coefficients were significant predictors of the count of convictions. The criminal history, education/employment, pro-crime attitudes, and anti-social patterns had significant, positive effects on convictions. These coefficients suggest that the experimental group subjects who had high scores on these four subscales posed significantly increased risk of recidivism.

Thus, the reentry program did not address these client issues sufficiently to prevent the recidivism that would be a natural consequence of these risk factors.

In addition to the identification of LS/CMI effects, we also found significant co-occurring disorder factors. The total mental health score of the CAAPE had a significant and positive effect on convictions as did a marijuana abuse profile. However, alcohol and stimulant abusers had significant negative effects on convictions. We also uncovered very important findings concerning the types of mental health disorders–five of the nine disorder types had significant effects on recidivism–some were positive and some were negative. There were three CAAPE mental disorders that had significant and positive consequences for recidivism: PTSD, obsessive/compulsive, and anti-social personality. Experimental group subjects with these disorders accumulated a greater number of post-release recidivism. Alternatively, there were two CAAPE disorders, major depressive and manic, that were significantly associated with a lower count of post-release convictions.

These multivariate results across the LS/CMI and CAAPE scores are important to corrections administrators, clinicians, and community reentry service organizations. These factors represent serious underlying disorders that must be remediated in order to reduce the risk of recidivism.

In the present case, these risks as identified via both the LSCMI scores and specific CAAPE indicators did not seem to elicit targeted and highly specific reentry services to remediate these recidivism factors.

CHAPTER EIGHT

THE REENTRY PROCESS

Process Analysis

This research study included a process analysis component. The purpose of the process analysis was to generate findings that might provide important feedback concerning the program activity itself as opposed to just the recidivism outcomes. The present process analysis necessarily focused on program participation across the collaborative partners and measured the consistency of program delivery activities which were a clear prerequisite for successful implementation of the program and achievement of program goals. Through a variety of methods, we monitored the implementation of program services and the extent to which delivery of reentry services to the experimental group adhered to the protocol or program model originally developed. Further, a particular type of process analysis was required for this program evaluation. The project was complex owing to: (1) the nature of the program itself–both institutional and community-based venues; and (2) the fact that it was a multi-agency collaboration with numerous staff participating. Given these factors, the research team determined that we needed to function as an action research partner across the two-year duration of the program and this approach was instituted from day one. The process analysis involved the monitoring and assessment of the following program activities by one or both members of the research team.

First, we read and assessed each and every email message that was sent to any program participant. Email messages were generated on an almost daily basis and such emails provided a snapshot of what was transpiring across the various activities. When problems were evident in the messages, we advised the participants, asked for clarification, and suggested possible remedies.

Second, we attended the monthly program meetings at Essex County Sheriff's Department (ECSD). The monthly meetings were crucial in establishing the status of the various stages of the program.

Third, we participated in the monthly conference calls with the Council of State Governments, the Technical Assistance advisors assigned by the Bureau of Justice Assistance to monitor the grant program.

Fourth, we participated in a site visit by the Council of State Governments. The site visit was extremely important to provide feedback to the Council of State Governments on the status of program milestones, problems encountered, and remedies contemplated.

Essentially, the research team functioned as real time, participant observers for all major activities of the program, regardless of which venue or which program partner was performing the activities. Figure 8-1 details the staff of the partners with whom the research team routinely interacted.

One member of the research team has been involved in criminal justice evaluations since 1977. It is important to note that he has never encountered professionals from criminal justice agencies, or from community-based partners, that were as cooperative to the research team, or as willing to let research-based considerations drive the process, than the staff of this program. We acknowledge the exemplary cooperation of the entire staff at the Middleton House of Correction across all levels of the administrative structure. The Assistant Superintendent, Leah Zanotti, was especially helpful. She provided ongoing assistance that was invaluable to the project. Further, the institutional staff had to provide extensive technical support in the form of weekly inmate rosters, controlled inmate movements to make them available for assessments, and other accommodations. The process analysis results are depicted below by functional area.

Planning Stage

All BJA Second Chance Act grants are required to have a Planning Stage which must be completed prior to the Implementation Stage. Grantees must follow a Planning and Implementation Guide which contains a series of exercises. Completion of the planning and implementation guide, in partnership with the technical assistance provider assigned by the National Reentry Resource Center (NRRC), is an eligibility requirement set by the Bureau of Justice Assistance (BJA) for jurisdictions to move from the planning phase, and receive funds, to begin the implementation phase of the grant. Essentially, the present grant began on 1 November 2014. The planning stage was facilitated by monthly meetings at ECSD among the grant partners and by conference calls with Council of State Governments (NRRC TA provider for the grant). The monthly meetings were well organized; were well run with a specific agenda; and were well attended. However, the research team identified one significant concern with respect to the planning process. Quite simply, the planning stage was too lengthy and extended from November 2014, to September 2015 (i.e., the point when exercises 1-13 in the Guide were scheduled for submission to BJA and the NRRC TA). In a short, two-year grant program like this COD reentry program, the length of the mandated planning process dramatically affected the implementation stage of the grant as detailed below. It would seem advisable, therefore, that grantees in two-year as opposed to three-year grants, should be required to complete all planning activities in a four to six-month (maximum) time frame.

Figure 8-1. COD Program Partners

Essex County Sheriff's Department	**Partner 1 Clinical Services**	**Partner 2 Reentry Services**
Assistant Superintendent, Grants Management	Clinical Supervisor, Agency Headquarters	Supervisor, Agency Headquarters
Assistant Superintendent, Programs and Reentry	Supervisor, ECSD	Case Manager Supervisor 1
Assistant Superintendent, Director of Communications	Director 1, TRAC	Case Manager Supervisor 2
Research Analyst	Director 2, TRAC	Case Manager 1
Four Program Staff	Discharge Coordinator 1	Case Manager 2
	Discharge Coordinator 2	Case Manager
	Discharge Coordinator 3	IT Specialist
	Seven Program Staff	Seven Program Staff

Implementation Stage

Risk Assessment Scoring Matrix

The planning issue that affected the various aspects of implementation was that the clinicians did not finalize the scoring matrix for the determination of co-occurring disorders in a timely manner. Although the original Program Narrative of the grant had not identified which specific assessment tool would be used to diagnosc co-occurring disorders, the CAAPE was selected early in the planning process. However, the Scoring Matrix for the CAAPE was not finalized until 24 August 2015, a period of ten months after the grant started. The researchers thereafter had to empirically test the reliability of the CAAPE across the staff who would be administering the instrument. The researchers determined on 17 September 2015, that reliability had been achieved. The CAAPE was then cleared for actual use on 21 September 2015 (11 months after the grant started).

Random Assignment to Experimental Groups

Because the scoring matrix was not developed and authorized for program use until 21 September 2015, the determination of case eligibility and then random assignment to the experimental and control groups was severely delayed. The first CAAPE was administered on 21 September 2015, and the last was administered on 9 December 2015. Thus, the composition of the two experimental groups was not finalized until late December 2015. This process was thus delayed and precious time to administer the CAAPE and select cases for inclusion in the grant was concomitantly delayed.

Experimental Group LS/CMI

Following random assignment to the experimental group and control group, the experimental group subjects had to be assessed via the LS/CMI, which in concert with the scores from the CAAPE, became the basis for the Discharge Plan that would guide the reentry process. In turn the discharge plan informed the service goals that were targeted for reentry services. Because of the earlier delays, both of these processes had to occur quite quickly over a relatively short period of time.

Experimental Group Release to the Community

The cumulative effect of the accumulated delays can be best evidenced with respect to the release dates for the experimental group. The earliest release occurred on 1 November 2015, while the latest happened on 21 April 2016 (the dates were virtually the same for the control group). The delayed release dates thus reduced the time for which subjects would be at risk in the community for the measurement of recidivism. Thus, the recidivism rates in this program might be even higher if all cases had a one-year follow-up period. BJA might consider a minimal investment of funds to do a follow-up study of recidivism for which all subjects had a one-year period at risk.

Risk Assessment, Discharge Planning, and Service Goals

Highly significant, if not the most significant, aspects of this study concern the following:

- Determination of client risk for recidivism based on the scores from the LS/CMI and the CAAPE;
- Use of discharge plans based on the assessment of risks; and
- Development of the service goals upon community reentry.

These three functions are interdependent parts of the reentry process. The process analysis monitored these activities very carefully and produced the following findings.

First, the researchers firmly believe that the staff of the clinical partner working within the ECSD facility (conducting LS/CMI assessments and developing discharge plans), and the staff of the community services partner (working within the facility to administer CAAPE assessments and then provide services in the community), made good faith efforts to perform these functions professionally. There is no question whatsoever concerning the commitment of staff to the project.

Second, however, there appear to have been issues beyond the control of the partners which may have affected the achievement of these functions. Due to personnel changes, the clinical partner had three different discharge coordinators, two of whom participated significantly in the LS/CMI and discharge planning processes. Any time there is personnel turnover like this, the reliability and consistency across the various staff is always a concern. Likewise, the community services partner had two different case manager supervisors and four different case managers providing community services. The community partner provided the researchers with data on the time lag between release and delivery of first services. These data ranged from mere days to a few weeks, but also a few months. While a delay of a few days or even weeks may not be crucial, a delay of a few months seriously jeopardized the reentry process. The community partner provided all the researchers with weekly updates on client service delivery. They were quite diligent in detailing the goal addressed and the means thereof. It is clear, however, that some clients were difficult to manage–they were hard to find initially, and ultimately reluctant to receive services.

Third, it must be remembered that this was a group of offenders at high risk and who had extensive co-occurring disorders as well as significant recidivism risks as detailed by the LS/CMI scores. It was noted in Chapter Seven's descriptive analyses, that the overall score and the eight subscales were higher for the experimental group recidivists, thus indicating a clinical diagnosis of greater problems than the experimental group subjects that did not recidivate. It was further indicated that the overall score, family/marital issues, and pro-crime attitude subscale were significantly higher for the recidivists. Further, the recidivist subset had a greater risk of recidivism for all the criminal history factors: greater prior arrests, longer time served, and were younger. Most important, the experimental recidivists had a significantly higher number of prior convictions, which we have seen was definitively related to recidivism in this evaluation for all cases (Chapter Six). Chapter Seven also indicated that the experimental recidivists had higher CAAPE scores for all five measures which reflects more extensive co-occurring disorders although these differences were not significant.

Beyond these descriptive data, we also reported in Chapter Seven that the results across the LS/CMI and CAAPE scores were predictive of recidivism, and thus, should be considered very important to corrections administrators, clinicians, and community reentry service organizations. These factors all represented serious underlying disorders that must be remediated in order to reduce the risk of recidivism. It would be expected, therefore, that these clinical indicators would lead to highly focused discharge planning so that reentry services would be tailored to these high-risk cases. Available information would suggest that this did not happen well enough. The service goals seemed quite generic and did not appear to be sufficiently tailored to the individual risk profiles observed across the experimental group subjects. We detail this issue further below. One of the researchers monitored the discharging planning very carefully. Three sample discharge plans as well as a blank template were examined. We advised the partners that there were numerous issues that we needed them to address. Below are the issues we raised (indented and italicized) and the replies from the partners (quotations and indented). Our commentary on each exchange is shown via regular text.

> *First, the discharge plan appears to be almost entirely inmate driven. While inmate responses should certainly contribute to the discharge process to provide a qualitative aspect from the client's point of view, the discharge plans do not appear to be done in any clinical manner. We were expecting that the discharge plans would be based on an assessment of the inmate's actual risks and actual needs, not his own perceptions. Thus, besides asking the inmate his concerns and needs, what is the clinical basis of the discharge plans?*

> "The initial basic assessment is mostly inmate driven. We do not have access to their criminal history and learning about their entire history whether it be medical, substance using, family etc. is based on the information that that client provides to us. A main part of clinical work is meeting the client where they are at which is the approach that we are using at the time being. The discharge planning for reentry ranking is based on both the LS/CMI and where the client ranked highly in as well as a basis of basic needs for every human being. We go through the LS/CMI summary page with each client explaining to them what it means to rank high or low in an area and how each category can be changed by different behaviors."

It did not make much sense to us that the clinical partner would allow the inmate to drive the needs assessment process because extensive information was available, including prior criminal history, commitment offense, CAAPE scores, and LS/CMI scores. So, we pursued these topics specifically.

> *Second, we were expecting that risks and needs would come from the CAAPEs and the LS/CMIs. We already know that one of the partners developed scoring matrices for the CAAPE. And it is our understanding that the LS/CMI has a few scales and forms that provide information about what the inmate actually needs and what his risks are. Thus, we need to know:*

> *How the CAAPEs are contributing to the determination of risks and needs assessment and thus affecting the discharge plans?*

How the LS/CMIs are contributing to the determination of risks and needs assessment and thus affecting the discharge plans?

If the CAAPEs and LS/CMIs are not being used, why not. And, why in that case were they even administered.

"We have not had access to the CAAPEs and scoring. The discharge plans (regarding the treatment plan and risk needs/assessments) have been based primarily off of the LS/CMI's results with additional input from the client if/when necessary. The discharge plans have been shared with the community service provider prior to each meeting they hold with a client and are used as either a basis to their assessment or a tool to fill in any holes they might have. The services provider compares their assessments with the initial results of the CAAPEs."

The reply to our second concern was problematic. The CAAPE scores were readily available to all partners as was a host of other data as indicated above concerning the first issue we raised. So, we tried again to zero in on the discharge plans.

Third, the inmates are able to select five areas they deem are most needed. Instead, should not the LS/CMI [and CAAPEs] be what tells us the needs of the inmate – not the inmates own view. Suppose they are in denial of their co-occurring disorder, or do not even know what their problems are exactly.

"This is primarily where the LS/CMI has been used (excluding housing which the LS/CMI does not account for but is a basic, highly important need for many of the clients)."

Fourth, moreover, what happens in the areas they don't designate as important? Do we not help them with those at all? They may be purposely avoiding mentioning the most problematic areas because they do not want to face the work involved.

"Clients are informed at the time when they meet with me that at any time should they feel that they need further assistance in any area or service they are to contact me (if they are still at Middleton) or contact their caseworker if they have been released. If the designated area was not a high mark on the LS/CMI it is typically left out unless a client specifies differently or changes their perception of needs. In which, at that point, all parties available work to meet the needs."

Fifth, we fail to see in the discharge plans where the community services provider can use the plans to offer their services upon release. It is not

> *clearly spelled out how the information in these packets equates to services.*
>
> "Within the discharge planning reentry ranking form and the discharge/transition plan form the basic needs provided by the LS/CMI and the client are found here. Each category is an area of which reentry services are needed. We have an additional form as part of the LS/CMI which clarifies the highly ranked sections and what each intervention would be. All this information is given to the provider prior to their assessment of the client."
>
> *In conclusion, the discharge plans form the basis of reentry services – the penultimate aspect for the experimental group. In order to evaluate the effectiveness of the program, we need to know how the risks and needs CLINICALLY ASSESSED translate into a discharge plan and THEN how that discharge plan translates into services completed by the provider.*
>
> "The risks and needs of each client has been assessed by the use of the LS/CMI. The LS/CMI is used to form the discharge/transition plan. The treatment/discharge plan is used to assist the service provider assessment which is then compared with the CAAPE. Services are then addressed with each client by their caseworker."

The preceding exchange between the researchers and the clinical partner convinced us that there was an effort to clinically assess the needs of the inmates in the experimental group using the LS/CMI and the inmates own self-evaluation. However, we do not believe that the very important CAAPE scores were used in any significant manner. Thus, we believe that the reentry services provided to clients were mostly generic and not at all targeted to the risk areas identified by the CAAPE scores. Thus, the CAAPE had identified inmates with particular mental health issues and specific substance abuse problems but these did not seem to be reflected in the services rendered.

This was a Second Chance Act program targeting offenders who had co-occurring disorders as reflected in the CAAPE scale scores. Thus, the CAAPE had to be included in the risk / needs assessment which lead to the discharge plan, and in turn, which lead to the reentry services that would be provided. We do not believe that the CAAPE scores were used to achieve as comprehensive a discharge plan as would have been achieved if the CAAPE was an integral part of the discharge process.

Process Analysis Summary

Overall, the process analysis was a valuable component in this research. Through the day-to-day monitoring of all aspects of the program, the process analysis generated the following major findings.

The Essex County Reentry Program for Adult Offenders with Co-Occurring Disorders was a diligent and committed effort to address the reentry needs and recidivism risks of an experimental group of subjects who received reentry services. The program was staffed by dedicated professionals, both within and without the institution.

Unfortunately, the success of the program was likely diminished by several factors that must be avoided in future reentry programs.

First, planning stage was entirely too long and necessarily delayed important aspects of the program. In fact, the planning stage was so long that implementation activities did not occur until ten months after the grant started.

Second, this delay lead to a series of other delays which compromised the potential of the program to render significant effects on the recidivism outcome.

The scoring matrix for the CAAPE was not developed early enough in the planning stage which caused ripple effects throughout the implementation stage. Because the scoring matrix was not developed and authorized for program use until 21 September 2015, the determination of case eligibility and then random assignment to the experimental and control groups was severely delayed. The first CAAPE was administered on 21 September 2015, and the last was administered on 9 December 2015. Thus, the composition of the two experimental groups was not finalized until late December 2015.

Following random assignment to the experimental group and control group, the experimental group subjects had to be assessed via the LS/CMI, which in concert with the scores from the CAAPE, became the basis for the Discharge Plan that would guide the reentry process. In turn the discharge plan informed the service goals that were targeted for reentry services. Because of the earlier delays, both of these processes had to occur quite quickly over a relatively short period of time.

The cumulative effect of all the delays can be best evidenced with respect to the release dates for the experimental group. The earliest release occurred on 1 November 2015, while the latest happened on 21 April 2016 (the dates were virtually the same for the control group). The delayed release dates thus reduced the time that subjects would be at risk in the community for the measurement of recidivism. Thus, the recidivism rates in this program might be even higher if all cases had a one-year follow-up period.

Third, the community-based services that were derived from the LS/CMI and CAAPE risk assessment tools and then the discharge plans, appeared to be more generic service goals rather than individual-specific service goals reflective of the serious underlying disorders present in many of the experimental subjects. We found little evidence that the co-occurring disorders of the experimental group were addressed in any clinically sufficient fashion.

CHAPTER NINE

PUNISHMENT PENDULUM

Introduction

In this chapter we intended to summarize the state of our knowledge with respect to prisoner reentry generally, and with respect to offenders with co-occurring disorders in particular. It has been almost 20 years since Petersilia (1999, 2001) and Travis (2000) sounded the warning alarm about prisoner reentry. It is highly desirable, therefore, to take stock of the progress which has been made to return offenders to the community with as low a probability of re-offending as possible. In fact, the National Reentry Resource Center, which was established in 2008 by the Second Chance Act (Public Law 110-199) and is administered by the U.S. Department of Justice's Bureau of Justice Assistance, recognized this situation in a recent publication, "Making People's Transition from Prison and Jail to the Community Safe and Successful: A Snapshot of National Progress in Reentry," 2017). There are two issues raised therein that deserve attention.

First, the National Reentry Resource Center (2017: 2) noted that:

> One of the most significant developments in criminal justice policy over the past 15 years has been a fundamental shift in thinking about the primary purpose of prisons and jails. Not long ago, elected officials saw the principal responsibility of corrections administrators as providing for the care, custody, and control of people who are incarcerated. Today, there is widespread agreement that government has a responsibility to ensure that when people are released to the community from jail or prison, they are less likely to reoffend than they were at the start of their sentence.

While we agree that there have been major sentencing and corrections developments over the past fifteen years, we believe that the 15-year window is entirely too short and fails to account for significant developments prior to 2002 which were the actual forces behind recent developments and the problems the criminal justice system faces today concerning prisoner reentry. What factors led to a shift in thinking about the primary purpose of prisons and jails? Did these factors emerge at a specific juncture, or were these factors the result of long-term developments? We believe that a more historical account is needed to understand properly the current situation. Simply, one cannot take a snapshot using an arbitrary point in time and hope to uncover the real driving forces. To the contrary, a longitudinal analysis is required.

Second, the National Reentry Resource Center (2017: 2) also suggested that:

> Although no single event is associated with this change in philosophy, a key milestone stands out. Late in 2004, Congress set to work on the Second Chance Act, which the House and Senate later passed with overwhelming bipartisan support. Elected officials in the nation's capital had made clear that ensuring people's safe and successful transition from prison and jail to the community wasn't a partisan issue, but simply good, smart policy—because anything short of that objective compromises public safety, wastes taxpayer dollars, and undermines the well-being and stability of communities.

BJA's identification of the *Second Chance Act* is likewise shortsighted. What were the driving forces behind the Act? Why did Congress entertain passage of this Act in 2004, and not for example, in 1994 or 1998 or any particular year for that matter? We believe once again that a much longer-range view is needed to grasp the dynamics of the environment in which the Act was passed. Thus, this chapter evolved into an analysis of important historical developments in penology which are crucial for an understanding of current issues–especially reentry. Chapter 10 will cover the current status of prisoner reentry.

The Pendulum of American Penology

Punishment Systems

The Pennsylvania System

The history of American penology reveals that there were differing philosophies concerning both the form and function of prisons. What was in vogue at one time was replaced by an alternate philosophy, and then the process repeated itself–like a pendulum which swung back and forth between varying punishment theories. It was clearly not a process which saw a previous theory replaced by a second and then by a third (see Rothman, 1971).

The best example of this was the earliest American prison systems (see Hirsch, 1992, Johnson, 2000). The Walnut Street Prison in Philadelphia was created in 1790. It was an expansion of the previous Walnut Street Jail which opened in 1773. The Walnut Street Prison resulted from the work of the Quakers of Philadelphia who came up with the concept for what they called a penitentiary—a place where prisoners could reflect on their crime and become truly sorry for what they had done. Shortly after the American Revolution, a group of Quakers formed the Philadelphia Society for Alleviating the Miseries of Public Prisons, whose goal was made clear in its name. The group would later become known as the Pennsylvania Prison Society. In the years after the Revolution this group worked to encourage prison reform, and its efforts finally paid off in 1790 when the Walnut Street Jail became the first state penitentiary in the country. The Quakers believed that through reflection and repentance, inmates would give up crime and leave prison rehabilitated (http://law.jrank.org/pages/11192/Walnut-Street-Prison.html).

In order to accommodate the change, a new cellblock called the "Penitentiary House" was added to the jail. It was built in the courtyard of the existing structure and it included a series of small cells designed to hold individual prisoners. The cells and the corridors connecting them were designed to prevent prisoners from communicating with each other. Windows were high up (the cells had nine-foot high ceilings) and grated and louvered to prevent prisoners from looking onto the street. Each cell had a mattress, a water tap, and a privy pipe. Inmates were confined to their cells for the duration of their confinement. The only person they saw was the guard and then only briefly once a day. They were sometimes allowed to read in their cells, but for the most part they sat in solitude. The Quakers saw this solitary confinement not as a punishment but as a time for reflection and remorse. That was the reason the inmates were not put to work. Labor, said penitentiary proponents, would preoccupy the inmates and keep them from reflecting on their crimes (http://law.jrank.org/pages/11192/Walnut-Street-Prison.html).

The Walnut Street Prison became the model for what became known as the "Pennsylvania System" (solitary confinement) of prison design and philosophy. Other prisons built on the Pennsylvania model included a prison in Pittsburgh in 1821, the Eastern State Penitentiary (1821) in Philadelphia and the Trenton State Prison in New Jersey (1832). The concepts of solitary confinement and repentance were key components of prison life at these institutions, although some Pennsylvania System prisons did introduce labor to the inmates. Visitors from overseas who were interested in prison reform visited Walnut Street, Eastern State, and similar prisons to see how they operated and to gain knowledge about prison reform strategies.

The success of the Walnut Street Prison was short-lived despite the good intentions of the Quakers. The practical matter of housing prisoners became more pressing than the desire among prison officials to rehabilitate the inmates. Walnut Street became overcrowded and dirty, and there was no sign that isolated prisoners were being rehabilitated through solitude. By the 1830s, the prison had outlived its usefulness, and it was closed in 1835. Later it was razed, and a library now stands on the site.

The Silent or Congregate System

At the same time that the Pennsylvania Solitary Confinement System was developing an alternate system, known as the Silent System, was being developed in New York State. In 1821, a prison was opened in the small upstate New York town of Auburn. The Auburn prison used an individual cellblock architecture, required inmates to work 10 hours per day, six days per week. The prisoners could congregate together but could not speak to one another. Some prison reformers believed that by making the inmates work in an atmosphere free of corruption or criminal behavior, they would build new sets of values. The work would rehabilitate them because it would give them a sense of purpose, discipline, and order. This system became known as the "Auburn System," and it was followed in 1826 with the opening of the famous Sing Sing prison on the banks of the Hudson River (http://law.jrank.org/pages/11192/Walnut-Street-Prison.html).

For a variety of reasons, the Auburn system was deemed to have worked better at rehabilitating prisoners than the Pennsylvania system, and in the next century the Auburn system became the dominant prison system. Many prisons built to operate under the Pennsylvania System switched to the Auburn System. Vestiges of the Pennsylvania System exist in the philosophy of humane punishment, although no prison in the U.S. today would place anyone in near-total isolation except in extreme circumstances.

The Rehabilitation Model

Elmira Reformatory

After 50 years under the Auburn Silent System, New York corrections officials determined that the 19th century's penal philosophy of punishment through silence, obedience and labor did not rehabilitate criminals. The pendulum had now swung to a new approach–rehabilitation. The new approach was the Elmira Reformatory which was opened in 1876. Under the direction of Zebulon Reed Brockway, an experienced penal administrator and innovator, Elmira's goal would be the reform of the convict, and its methods would be psychological rather than physical. Instead of coercion through harsh punishments and enforced silence, Elmira would encourage rehabilitation with a reward system. The mass regimentation of Auburn would yield to scientific classification and individualized treatment. Instead of fixed sentences to fit the crime, the "indeterminate sentence" would be adjustable to fit the criminal. Rather than outright release after the offender "paid his debt to society," a new parole procedure would assure he did not return to his life of crime upon release (http://www.correctionhistory.org/html/chronicl/docs2day/elmira.html).

Brockway's correctional philosophy, and his deep reliance on the indeterminate sentence made him a perfect choice to be the Superintendent of the New Elmira Reformatory. He wrote:

> No man, be he judge, lawyer or layman, can determine beforehand the date when imprisonment shall work reformation in any case, and it is an outrage upon society to return to the privileges of citizenship those having proved themselves dangerous and bad by the commission of crime, until a cure is wrought and reformation reached, Such minimum of restraint must be retained, as will protect the people from their pernicious influence, which possibility will prove more powerfully deterrent upon criminals and the criminal class—than the severities of the inquisition possibly could. Therefore, as for the other reasons suggested, sentences should not be determinate bat indeterminate. By this is meant, (to state briefly) *that all persons in a State, who are convicted of crimes or offences before a competent court, shall he deemed wards of the State, and shall he committed to the custody of the Board of Guardians, until in their judgment they may he returned to society with ordinary safety and in accord with their own highest welfare* (Brockway, 1970: 8; emphasis in original).

Brockway instituted a modern classification system in his own office where he would interview each new arrival, probing into the offender's social, economic, psychological, biological and moral make-up, "until the subjective defect is apparently discovered," and then make a preliminary work and school assignment. Brockway placed the inmates in grades and reviewed their classification continuously. He encouraged cranial measurements and research into criminal types and developed special programs for what were called "defectives" (http://www.correctionhistory.org/html/chronicl/docs2day/elmira.html).

Elmira quietly redefined the term "reform," until then understood only in purely religious terms. Teaching rather than preaching, they downplayed religious conversion in favor of the more realistic goal of law-abiding behavior. The new reformatory generated tremendous excitement and pushed American corrections into the future. The core of Brockway's program: classification with gradations of freedom and privilege, along with an emphasis on development of the whole person, physical, intellectual, and spiritual remains at the basis of modern corrections.

Elmira's systemic focus on rehabilitation through individual treatment, the indeterminate sentence and parole were universally embraced and would not be seriously questioned until the 1970's, when a new concern for individual liberties and due process would begin to make inroads on the rehabilitative ideal. In New York and elsewhere, the indeterminate sentence and parole system had been attacked, and modified, in New York on the grounds that the administrative discretion and differential treatment necessary to administer it are inconsistent with principles of justice, a fact candidly acknowledged by Brockway (http://www.correctionhistory.org/html/chronicl/docs2day/elmira.html).

What Works? Nothing Works!

The rehabilitation, or medical model, enjoyed hegemony in corrections for almost exactly 100 years. It was, without a doubt, the dominant corrections model everywhere. Then, research studies began appearing which questioned the effectiveness, usefulness, fairness, etc., of the rehabilitation approach in corrections. For our purposes here, two such studies were notable.

First, Robison and Smith (1971) published their study which reviewed the results of numerous studies of corrections programs in California. They were attempting to address five significant questions surrounding alternate choices in offender processing. Their five questions were as follows:

1. Will they act differently if we lock them up rather than place them on probation?

2. Will they recidivate less if we keep them locked up longer?

3. Do educating and treating in prison reduce recidivism?

4. Does supervising them more closely in smaller parole caseloads reduce recidivism?

5. What difference does it make whether we discharge prisoners outright or supervise them on parole? (Robison and Smith, 1971: 68).

After a thorough review of numerous studies, Robison and Smith indicated that, the single answer, then, to each of the five questions originally posed–will the clients act differently if we lock them up, or keep them locked up longer, or do something with them inside, or watch them more closely afterward, or cut them loose officially–is "Probably not" (1971: 80). The Robison and Smith study provided very pessimistic findings about the rehabilitative model that was in use in California (and elsewhere) prisons in the 1960s. Perhaps the findings only pertained to California. Perhaps rehabilitation worked elsewhere. The answer would come soon enough.

Martinson (1974) and colleagues (Lipton, Martinson, and Wilks, 1975). conducted an even more rigorous study, internationally not just nationally. They employed a rigorous methodology to ensure that only valid comparative studies were included in the research.

First, they did a six-month search of the literature for any available reports published in the English language on rehabilitation efforts that had been made in American corrections systems and those of other countries from 1945 through 1967. Second, they then chose from that literature all those studies whose findings were interpretable–that is, whose design and execution met the conventional standards of social science research. They indicated the criteria were rigorous but hardly esoteric: (1) a study had to be an evaluation of a treatment method; (2) it had to employ an independent measure of the improvement secured by that method; and (3) it had to use some control group, some untreated individuals with whom the treated ones could be compared. Third, they excluded studies for the following conventional, methodological criteria:

- Insufficient data;

- Study was only preliminary;

- Study provided only a summary of findings and did not allow a reader to evaluate those findings;

- Results were confounded by extraneous factors;
- Use of unreliable measures;
- Obscure descriptions of the treatment in question;
- Spurious conclusions from the data;
- Samples were described poorly, were too small, or provided no comparability between treated and untreated groups;
- Used inappropriate statistical tests and did not provide enough information for the reader to recompute the data.

The result of this rigorous assessment was a total of 231 acceptable research studies which were analyzed but were presented in a manner which allowed a reader to do his/her own evaluations (Martinson, 1974: 24). Like Robison and Smith (1971). Martinson framed the article by posing relevant questions surrounding various rehabilitative techniques and then summarized what the research literature indicated. The questions posed by Martinson are given below and are numbered and double indented, while the answers are indented and italicized.

Education and Vocational Training

1. Isn't it true that a correctional facility running a truly rehabilitative program–one that prepares inmates for life on the outside through education and vocational training–will turn out more successful individuals than will a prison which merely leaves its inmates to rot?

   If this is true, the fact remains that there is very little empirical evidence to support it (Martinson, 1974: 25).

Effects of Individual Counseling

2. But when we speak of a rehabilitative prison, aren't we referring to more than education and skill development alone? Isn't what's needed some way of counseling inmates, or helping them with the deeper problems that have caused their maladjustment?

This, too, is a reasonable hypothesis; but when one examines the programs of this type that have been tried, it's hard to find any more grounds for enthusiasm than we found with skill development and education (Martinson, 1974: 29).

Transforming the Institutional Environment

3. But maybe the reason these counseling programs don't seem to work is not that they are ineffective per se, but that the institutional environment outside the program is unwholesome enough to undo any good work that the counseling does. Isn't a truly successful rehabilitative institution the one where the inmate's whole environment is directed towards true correction rather than towards custody or punishment?

   One study of such a program, by Robison (1967), found that the therapy did seem to reduce recidivism after one year. After two years, however, this effect disappeared, and the treated convicts did no better than the untreated. Another study by Kassebaum, Ward, and Wilner (1971), dealt with a program which had been able to effect an exceptionally extensive and experimentally rigorous transformation of the institutional environment. This sophisticated study had a follow-up period of 36 months, and it found that the program had no significant effect on parole failure or success rates (Martinson, 1974: 25).

Medical Treatment

4. Isn't there anything you can do in an institutional setting that will reduce recidivism, for instance, through strictly medical treatment?

   A number of studies deal with the results of efforts to change the behavior of offenders through drugs and surgery. As for surgery, the one experimental study of a plastic surgery program by Mandell (1967) had negative results. For non-addicts who received plastic surgery, Mandell purported to find improvement in performance on parole; but when one reanalyzes his data, it appears that surgery alone did not in fact make a significant difference (Martinson, 1974: 35).

The Effects of Sentencing

5. Well, at least it may be possible to manipulate certain gross features of the existing, conventional prison system–such as length of sentence and degree of security–in order to affect these recidivism rates. Isn't this the case?

   At this point, it's still impossible to say that this is the case. As for the degree of security in an institution, Glaser's (1964) work reported that, for both youth and adults, a less restrictive "custody grading" in American federal prisons was related to success on parole; but this is hardly surprising, since those assigned to more restrictive custody are likely to be worse risks in the first place (Martinson, 1974: 36).

Decarcerating the Convict

6. All of this seems to suggest that there's not much we know how to do to rehabilitate an offender when he's in an institution. Doesn't this lead to the clear possibility that the way to rehabilitate offenders is to deal with them outside an institutional setting?

   But by and large, when one takes the programs that have been administered in institutions and applies them in a non-institutional setting, the results do not grow to encouraging proportions (Martinson, 1974: 38).

Does Nothing Work?

7. Do all of these studies lead us irrevocably to the conclusion that nothing works, that we haven't the faintest clue about how to rehabilitate offenders and reduce recidivism? And if so, what shall we do?

   It is just possible that some of our treatment programs are working to some extent, but that our research is so bad that it is incapable of telling. Having entered this very serious caveat, I am bound to say that these data, involving over two hundred studies and hundreds of thousands of individuals as they do, are the best available and give us very little reason to hope that we have in fact found a sure way of reducing recidivism through rehabilitation. This is not to say that we found no instances of success or partial success; it is only to say that these instances have been isolated, producing no clear pattern to indicate the efficacy of any particular method of treatment (Martinson, 1974: 48-49).

The overall conclusions offered by Martinson, were even more discouraging concerning the value of the rehabilitative model of corrections than was the case with the Robison and Smith (1971) paper. Martinson and colleagues included many more studies and the focus was international. Martinson (1974: 49-50) offered three overriding conclusions.

1. It may be simply that our programs aren't yet good enough–that the education we provide to inmates is still poor education, that the therapy we administer is not administered skillfully enough, that our intensive supervision and counseling do not yet provide enough personal support for the offenders who are subjected to them. If one wishes to believe this, then what our correctional system needs is simply a more full-hearted commitment to the strategy of treatment.

2. It may be, on the other hand, that there is a more radical flaw in our present strategies–that education at its best, or that psychotherapy at its best, cannot overcome, or even appreciably reduce, the powerful tendency for offenders to continue in criminal behavior. Our present treatment programs are based on a theory of crime as a "disease"–that is to say, as something foreign and abnormal in the individual which can presumably be cured. This theory may well be flawed, in that it overlooks–indeed denies–both the normality of crime in society and the personal normality of a very large proportion of offenders, criminals who are merely responding to the facts and conditions of our society.

3. This opposing theory of "crime as a social phenomenon" directs our attention away from a "rehabilitative" strategy, away from the notion that we may best insure public safety through a series of "treatments" to be imposed forcibly on convicted offenders. These treatments have on occasion become, and have the potential for becoming, so draconian as to offend the moral order of a democratic society; and the theory of crime as a social phenomenon suggests that such treatments may be not only offensive but ineffective as well. This theory points, instead, to decarceration for low-risk offenders–and, presumably, to keeping high-risk offenders in prisons which are nothing more (and

aim to be nothing mote) than custodial institutions. But this approach has its own problems.

The Just Deserts Model

With all due respect to the position as articulated by the National Resource Reentry Center above, one of the most significant changes in the criminal justice system following the realization that nothing works was a swing of the pendulum away from rehabilitation and back towards punishment, and this time, towards a new justification for punishment–the "just deserts" philosophy. This rationale for punishment was not only unlike rehabilitation and so-called reformatories, it was also quite dissimilar to the punishment systems in the early prisons reviewed above. Among the criminologists who addressed the just deserts approach, Andrew von Hirsch occupies a preeminent status. In a series of journal articles and two major books (von Hirsch, 1976; 1987) he laid out the necessity for, and the principles of, a just deserts approach to criminal sentencing. We have neither sufficient space here, nor the substantive need to cover von Hirsch's two books in depth. We highly recommend that interested readers pursue a more in-depth analysis of his writings in both of these books.

Von Hirsch's first volume, *Doing Justice* (1976) evolved from the work of a *Committee for the Study of Incarceration* which was funded by the Field Foundation and the New World Foundation. Essentially, the committee was formed to consider the fundamental goals or purposes for criminal sentences, including whether prison was necessary. Members were chosen so as to represent a wide variety of disciplines to ensure diversity of opinions about the fundamental concepts surrounding punishment.

The committee examined the basic assumptions behind the dominant punishment paradigm as reflected in the Model Sentencing Act (National Council on Crime and Delinquency,1972: 9) which stated:

> Persons convicted of crime shall be dealt with in accordance with their potential for rehabilitation, considering their individual characteristics, circumstances, and needs....dangerous offenders shall be identified, segregated, and correctively treated in custody for as long terms as needed.

The committee identified the three main assumptions underlying the above viewpoint (von Hirsch, 1976: 9-10). First, there is the fundamental assumption that sanctions should not punish per se but should rehabilitate–the offender should receive the correctional treatment best suited to inculcate law-abiding habits. This is the medical model and requires that the choice of sentence and where it is carried out comport with the goal of rehabilitation.

Second, instead of a sanction based on the severity of the instant offense alone or in concert with prior record, the sanction should be based on the notion of predictive restraint–the likelihood of the offender returning to a life of crime.

Third, the quintessential requirement of the rehabilitation mode is that decision making must be individualized.

The specific sanction must be tailored to the offender's need for treatment and his/her risk for re-offending. This requires that courts and corrections officials be accorded wide discretion and latitude with as few constraints as possible.

Von Hirsch indicated that the rationale for punishment had heretofore consisted of: (1) deterrence, both specific and general; (2) restraint or selective incapacitation; (3) rehabilitation. All of these rationales must confront an allocation problem–how long to punish (and to an extent where). Thus, why should some offenders be punished longer or more harshly than others? Given that these goals are all utilitarian, and thus, the amount of punishment is tied to some metric of crimes prevented or persons reformed, the evidence is scarce or non-existent that these utility functions are being achieved. Therefore, the discretionary power accorded to various stages of the criminal justice system is unfair, unwarranted, and perhaps even biased.

As an alternative, von Hirsch and the committee offered the concept of "desert." Society should punish people because they engaged in conduct which is blameworthy and should be condemned. Desert thus looks backward at prior conduct and not speculatively forward regarding crimes that the offender may commit in the future. This orientation to the past distinguishes desert from the other purported aims of punishment (i.e., deterrence, incapacitation, rehabilitation) which seek to justify punishment by its presumed and prospective usefulness in preventing crime.

Von Hirsch (1976: 47) indicated that the committee based the desert concept on Emmanuel Kant's work. That is, in a social contract system, people essentially agree not to infringe on one another's rights and freedoms. Thus, a rule violator necessarily gains an advantage because he/she failed to conform while most others conform to the rules. Punishment, therefore, imposes a counterbalancing disadvantage on the violator to restore equilibrium–after undergoing the punishment, the violator ceases to have an advantage over his/her non-violating peers. Punishment necessarily includes a moral disapproval and conveys in dramatic fashion that the conduct was wrong and that the person is blameworthy for having committed it. The offender deserves the reprobation of punishment not only to restore equilibrium but also, he deserves blame for the wrongdoing.

In a just desert system of punishment, the allocation of penalties becomes preeminent over utilitarian concerns such as deterrence or incapacitation, or rehabilitation. A desert system only needs to consider: (1) the seriousness of the current offense; and (2) the number and seriousness of prior offenses. There is no speculation about future recidivism which necessarily entails false positives and false negatives which render differential sentences unfair and unjust. Criminals are punished only for what they have already done–not might do. Penalties are allocated for past wrongdoing not inaccurate or even false predictions about the future.

California Abolishes Determinate Sentencing (1976)

In 1976, California passed *The Determinate Sentencing Act* (Senate Bill 42, 1876). According to one informed observer, this was a criminal justice event of national significance (Johnson, 1978: 13). California had adopted the indeterminate sentence system in 1917, and later in 1944, created the Adult Authority (i.e., the Parole Board). California had thoroughly embraced the indeterminate sentence and “was famous or notorious as the state whose laws seemed most thoroughly committed to the idea that sentences should be indeterminate” (Johnson, 1978: 13). First, the length of the sentence should depend more on the individual characteristics of the criminal than on the nature of the crime. Second, maximum discretion over length of sentences should be given to an administrative agency shielded from public accountability. Third, purpose of imprisonment is to rehabilitate the offender and to protect society from his further misdeeds. Fourth, the released prisoner should be subjected to a lengthy period of parole supervision to protect the public and to insure his rehabilitation.

Essentially, the indeterminate sentence in California worked as follows. Judges would typically sentence convicted offenders to very broad-ranging prison terms (e.g., five years to life for armed robbery). After an inmate had served a certain minimum period amount of time, the adult authority would then determine the remaining sentence length. The parole board's decision was supposed to be influenced by how the inmate had behaved during his/her sentence and the demonstrated degree of "rehabilitation" (e.g., completing classes, job training, attending counseling, etc.).

So, what did the new determinate sentence statute do? According to Johnson the determinate sentencing law reflected the opposite assumptions in every respect compared to the rehabilitation model. First, it provided a relatively narrow range of fixed penalties for each crime. Second, it replaced the discretion of the parole board over release with a complex system of "good time" credits. Third, it greatly lessened the period of parole and the importance of parole supervision (1978: 14). By far, the most significant development concerned the purpose for punishment. Section 1 of *The Determinate Sentencing Act* amended California *Penal Code* Section 1170 as follows:

> "The Legislature finds and declares that the purpose of imprisonment for crime is punishment. This purpose is best served by terms proportionate to the seriousness of the offense with provision for uniformity in the sentences of offenders committing the same offense under similar circumstances. The Legislature further finds and declares that the elimination of disparity and the provision of uniformity of sentences can best be achieved by determinate sentences fixed by statute in proportion to the seriousness of the offense as determined by the Legislature to be imposed by the court with specified discretion."

Johnson (1978: 55), in the conclusion of his historical review of the passage of *The Determinate Sentencing Act* offers a few extremely important observations.

> One lesson is, perhaps, that the struggle between "just deserts" and "social defense" as means to provide public satisfaction and protection through sentencing is far from over. The move toward "indeterminacy" in the earlier part of this century was widely interpreted, after the fact, as a move toward "social defense" –reformed inmates would be quickly released, unreformed inmates retained, both by a board of "experts." To be sure, "just deserts," both as proportionate and as uniform was also to be served, though it was never clear just how except as "proportionate" came to mean in accordance with the degree of rehabilitation and risk.
>
> The move toward "determinacy" is being interpreted as a move toward "just deserts"–defendants will be punished equally in accordance with the moral and material damage they have wrought. But the "indeterminate sentence" never worked as advertised, the "experts" continuing mainly to issue terms consonant with their vision of "just deserts," although leavened, to be sure, by their fears about what prisoners might do if released.

> Nor are the differing implications of "just deserts" and "social defense" all that are involved; each contains its own difficulties. There is little sign that the various interested parties agree what "deserts" are "just" for different offenses or, above all, different offenders. Nor is there any sign that agreement can be reached about which offenders truly represent a serious future risk, without making more mistakes than many find acceptable. And even if the number of mistakes could be reduced, there are many who would still hold that preventive detention is immoral if not unconstitutional and should not be practiced.

But, perhaps Johnson's most prophetic observation was the following, "None of these controversies will go away as a result of the new law; the legislature's hope, if members seriously thought about it, can only be to have defused them temporarily" (1978: 55). And, it was temporary.

Only two years after *The Determinate Sentencing Act* was passed, Governor Brown signed a mandatory parole law that increased the time prisoners must be supervised after prison from one year to three. Further, determinate sentencing enabled lawmakers to pass hundreds of increasingly stricter sentences for crimes. Mandatory three-year parole bounced so many felons back behind bars on violations that by 2006 they accounted for two-thirds of annual prison admissions, (St. John, 2014). More just deserts.

California Three Strikes Law

In 1994, voters passed the ultimate just deserts policy. In June 1992, 18-year-old Kimber Reynolds, upon leaving a local restaurant, was attacked by two men. They tried to grab her purse and ultimately shot her in the ear with a .357 magnum. She died 26 hours later. Her father, Mike Reynolds, made her a promise on her deathbed: "I promised her that if I could do anything to prevent this from happening to other kids, I would do everything I could." The men responsible for the murder of Kimber were repeat offenders which led Mike Reynolds to his campaign to keep repeat offenders behind bars. Eighteen months after the death of Kimber Reynolds, 12-year-old Polly Klaas was kidnaped, raped and murdered by Richard Allen Davis, also a repeat offender (National Public Radio, 2009).

The Three Strikes Law was designed to increase prison sentences for repeat offenders. The three-strikes sentencing model was enacted as follows (Ballotpedia.org, 1994):

- Strike 1: persons with no prior violent or serious felony conviction who commit a violent or serious felony receive a sentence for that felony as prescribed by state law.

- Strike 2: persons with one prior violent or serious felony conviction who again commit any type of felony receive a sentence twice the term state law otherwise required.

- Strike 3: persons with two prior violent or serious felony convictions who again commit any type of felony receive a life sentence, with a minimum imprisonment of 25 years.

The three strikes law also contained specific just deserts mechanisms (Vitiello, 1997):

- Consecutive Sentencing
  - The statute requires consecutive, rather than concurrent, sentencing for multiple offenses committed by strikers. For example, an offender convicted of two third strike offenses would receive a minimum term of 50 years (two 25-year terms added together) to life.

- *Unlimited Aggregate Term*
  - There is no limit to the number of felonies that can be included in the consecutive sentence.

- *Time Since Prior Conviction Not Considered*
  - The length of time between the prior and new felony conviction does not affect the imposition of the new sentence, so serious and violent felony offenses committed many years before a new offense can be counted as prior strikes.

- *Probation, Suspension, or Diversion Prohibited*
  - Probation may not be granted for the new felony, nor may imposition of the sentence be suspended for any prior offense. The defendant must be committed to state prison and is not eligible for diversion.

- *Prosecutorial Discretion*
  - Prosecutors can move to dismiss, or to strike prior felonies from consideration during sentencing in the furtherance of justice,

- *Limited Good Time Credits*
    - Strikers cannot reduce the time they spend in prison by more than one-fifth (rather than the standard of one-half) by earning credits from work or education activities.

Following the passage of three strikes, the inevitable tinkering commenced. The state was struggling with the effects of determinate sentencing and the three strikes law–too much just deserts? Proposed changes were put on the ballot for voter consideration in 2000, 2004, 2012, and 2014. In 2000, Proposition 36 was certified for the ballot. The initiative was designed to require probation and drug treatment for persons convicted of being under the influence of controlled substances and similar parole violations, rather than be subject to the provisions of Proposition 184. Voters approved Proposition 36, with 60.86 percent in favor. In 2004, voters rejected Proposition 66, which would have removed non-serious and non-violent felonies from counting as Strike 3 under Proposition 184. Governor Schwarzenegger opposed Proposition 66 and it failed. In 2012, voters approved Proposition 36, which amended Proposition 184 to exclude non-serious and non-violent felonies, except those involving firearms, sex offenses, or drug offenses, from counting as Strike 3. The initiative authorized judges to re-sentence people sentenced to life imprisonment under Proposition 184 for third offenses that were non-serious and non-violent. In 2014, Proposition 47 was passed by California voters on November 4. It reduced certain drug possession felonies to misdemeanors. It also required misdemeanor sentencing for petty theft, receiving stolen property and forging/writing bad checks when the amount involved is $950 or less.

Clearly, the three strikes law was ill conceived. We are not aware of any competent empirical evidence that the third offense represents the most propitious intervention point for a selective incapacitation strategy. None of the major studies available at the time–not the famous Philadelphia Birth Cohort studies, Wolfgang, Figlio, and Sellin, 1972; Wolfgang, Thornberry, and Figlio, 1987, Tracy, Wolfgang, and Figlio. 1990–nor the famous National Academy of Sciences Panel on Career Criminals, Blumstein, Cohen, Roth, and Visher, 1986–nor the famous Rand Inmate Surveys, Visher, 1986–would have supported the third offense as the best intervention point. To the contrary, available evidence would have suggested the fifth or sixth offense as the earliest point for selective incapacitation. So why did California choose a Three Strikes Law? The answer is obvious.

Let's Change the Name of the Department

By the time Governor Schwarzenegger took office in 2003, California prisons were a mess. Federal investigations, out-of-control costs, accusations of abuse, substandard prisoner healthcare and allegations of a code of silence among guards to stymie investigations had played out in the media for years. Shortly after taking office, Governor Schwarzenegger tapped the man who had been governor during the prison system's greatest expansion (1983-1991), George Deukmejian, to chair an independent review of the prison system. The panel's report documented the collapse of the system following three decades of a radical, voter-directed transformation that included hundreds of new sentencing laws, 22 new prisons, and dismantling of most rehabilitative programs. The Governor's Reorganization Plan (Chapter 10, Statutes of 2005) was signed into law by Governor Schwarzenegger in May 2005, creating the California Department of Corrections and Rehabilitation (CDCR) on July 1, 2005.

Just like that, the punishment pendulum was symbolically swung back towards rehabilitation. *Inside CDCR*, the Newsletter of the department, offered the following concerning the reorganization (Inside CDCR, 2015), "The addition of the word 'rehabilitation' to our department's name was significant. It is not enough to incarcerate; one of our core public safety missions is to give inmates opportunities to live productive, law-abiding lives through programs that better prepare them for their return to our communities. CDCR's heavy investments in rehabilitation are paying off," said CDCR Secretary Jeff Beard. "We now have a network of reentry hubs, and we are rebuilding our training, education and substance abuse programs to make the 'R' in CDCR a reality." "A reorganized Department of Corrections and Rehabilitation will flatten the organization structure of the youth and adult correctional system, directly connecting the top layer of management with every aspect of the organization's performance," the press release states. "It will more clearly define the authority and responsibilities of key managers and will empower them to carryout out their assigned responsibilities. ... Finally, it will enable the Secretary to enact meaningful change throughout the entire organization to make it more effective, efficient and accountable. This is an important departure from the past."

Of course, whether adding "rehabilitation" to the name of the department, and the associated changes that will need to be implemented to help CDCR move away from punishment and back to rehabilitation, do in fact lead to effective rehabilitation and lower recidivism is an empirical question. Since the above comments came in 2015, ten years after the name change, the newsletter should have incorporated some recidivism data to show the progress made. So, we hunted down these data ourselves. The recidivism data are examined below.

Federal Sentencing Reform Act (1984)

The federal government followed California's lead and implemented its own determinate sentencing system. *The Sentencing Reform Act of 1984* (Title II of the Comprehensive Crime Control Act of 1984) established the United States Sentencing Commission and delegated to it authority to promulgate sentencing guidelines for the federal courts. After a period of intensive review and empirical study of the sentencing process, the Commission issued initial guidelines that took effect on November 1, 1987 (United States Sentencing Commission, 1991). The guidelines were promulgated in 1987, but district and circuit court rulings prevented their full implementation until the Supreme Court, in *Mistretta v. United States*, 488 U.S. 361 (1989), affirmed the constitutionality of the Commission and its work in crafting sentencing guidelines.

There are numerous accounts of the historical underpinnings, legislative intents, and accounts of the early years of the federal sentencing guidelines. The reader is referred to these writings (Nagel, 1990, Howell, 2004; United States Sentencing Commission, 2004). For our purposes, the following is sufficient to capture the effects on offender reentry.

The Sentencing Reform Act of 1984 created a new era of sentencing in federal courts. Prior to the implementation of the reforms, federal crimes carried very broad ranges of indeterminate penalties, and federal judges had wide discretion to choose the sentence they felt would be most appropriate. Judges were not required to explain the reasons for the sentence imposed, and the sentences were largely immune from appeal. Like in California, the time actually served by most offenders was determined by the Parole Commission, and offenders, on average, served just 58 percent of the sentences that had been imposed. The sentencing process which is a critical component of the criminal justice process, was opaque, undocumented, and largely discretionary. Because of its impenetrability to outside observers, there was a sense that the process was unfair, disparate, and ineffective for controlling crime (United States Sentencing Commission, 2004: iv). The rationale for the sentencing system was predicated on "coercive rehabilitation" and sentences were based on the judge ordering a long sentence and then the parole board granting release based on sufficient rehabilitation (*Mistretta*: 363; Hatch, 1993: 187).

In order to inject transparency, consistency, and fairness into the sentencing process, Congress passed *The Sentencing Reform Act* which established the U.S. Sentencing Commission and charged it with establishing guidelines for federal sentencing. The Act established the following goals for sentencing reform:

- To reflect the seriousness of the offense, to promote respect for the law, and to provide just punishment for the offense;
- To afford adequate deterrence to criminal conduct;
- To protect the public from further crimes of the defendant; and
- To provide the defendant with needed educational or vocational training, medical care, or other correctional treatment in the most effective manner (28 U.S.C. § 991(b)(1)).

In order to accomplish these goals, the Act:

- Abolished determinate sentencing.
- Abolished parole.
- Instituted fixed sentences based on crime severity and prior criminal history.
- Required offenders to serve 85 percent of the guideline sentence (reflective of statutory "good time" equal to 54 days per year).

Although the goals of the Act. to eliminate disparity and create a system that was fair, transparent, and consistent. are all quite laudatory, there is an aspect of the Act that was most unfortunate. That is, Howell has noted that the Act introduced a new comprehensive scheme for structuring judicial sentencing discretion that drastically altered sentencing in the federal criminal justice system and was designed to eliminate sentencing disparity, but in doing so, Congress specifically rejected the notion of rehabilitation as a primary sentencing objective (Howell, 2004: 1072; see also Hatch, 1993: 188). The United States Sentencing Commission's own report (2004:13) makes it clear that rehabilitation is a low priority aspect of the Act:

> Rehabilitation. The SRA directs judges to consider each defendant's need for educational and treatment services when imposing sentence. However, the SRA and the guidelines make rehabilitation a lower priority than other sentencing goals (see Hofer and Allenbaugh, 2003). For example, the Commission was directed to ensure that "the guidelines reflect the inappropriateness of imposing a sentence to a term of imprisonment for the purpose of rehabilitating the defendant." 28 U.S.C. § 994(k). Despite the relatively low priority given rehabilitation, judges are still required to assess a defendant's need for treatment or training when they decide whether to impose any special conditions of probation or supervised release. See USSG §5D1.3(d). (Supervised release has replaced parole as the means to provide offenders with post-imprisonment supervision.)

Thus, *The Sentencing Reform Act* was designed to swing the pendulum away from rehabilitation towards so called just punishment. Whether anticipated or not, the effects were decisive. The United States Sentencing Commission report for 1991, often referred to as the "four-year evaluation," indicated three significant effects.

First, the mean sentence lengths across all offenses nearly doubled, increasing from 24 months in July 1984 to 46 months in June 1990 and these increases in the average terms of imprisonment reflect statistically significant impacts of three major interventions–the Anti-Drug Abuse Act of 1986, the initial implementation of the guidelines, and the Mistretta decision.

Second, overall, mean prison terms for drug offenders increased throughout the study period from 27 months in July 1984 to 67 months in June 1990, an increase of 248 percent.

Third, the average prison terms for robbery offenders also increased over the study period. Increases primarily occurred after initial guideline implementation and the Mistretta decision; both interventions produced significant positive changes–mean sentences for robbery offenses were 60 months in July 1984 and rose to 78 months in June 1990 (United States Sentencing Commission, 1991: 60).

Overall, the four-year evaluation indicated that the sentencing guidelines is a punishment system that, between 1984 and 1990, experienced significant increases both in the use of incarcerative sentences and in the average length of prison sentences (United States Sentencing Commission, 1991: 63).

Similarly, the 15-year evaluation indicated that, on average, federal offenders received substantially more severe sentences under the guidelines than they did in the pre-guidelines era. Between 1987and 1989, the first year in which the majority of federal offenders were sentenced under the guidelines, the average prison time expected to be served almost doubled. By 1992, the average time in prison had more than doubled, from 26 months in 1986 to 59 months in 1992. Since fiscal year 1992 there was a slight and gradual decline in average prison time, but federal offenders sentenced in 2002 will still spend about twice as long in prison as did offenders sentenced prior to passage of *The Sentencing Reform Act* (United States Sentencing Commission, 2004: 46).

Just two years after the full implementation of *The Sentencing Reform Act* the warden of a federal correctional institution published an article that raised some interesting observation. Warden Luttrell noted that the Act would affect prison management in a number of ways. First, since parole was abolished and good time was statutorily regulated, inmates realized that they had little to lose for misconduct (1991: 55). Second, inmates would serve longer sentences. the inmate population would become older, and the inmate population would increase thus affecting inmate management and programming. As we show below, he was quite right.

Sentencing Reform and Inmate Population

The sentencing reforms in California and at the federal level came during a period of rising crime rates and increasing incarceration rates as detailed in Chapter One. This was perhaps not the best time to abandon rehabilitation. Table 9-1 captures the relationship between the sentencing reforms and the changes in the inmate population in California and the Bureau of Prisons.

In California, the prison population increased 723 percent from 1978 to 2006. During this period several reforms were instituted. First, rehabilitation was abandoned and determinate sentencing was implemented in 1978. Between 1978 and 1994, when Three Strikes was passed, the prison population increased 491 percent. Second, despite this startling increase in the prison population as of 1994, California passed Three Strikes and the inmate population rose another 35 percent as of 2005. Finally, in 2005 California changed the name and the focus of the corrections department to the California Department of Correction and Rehabilitation.

At the federal level, the inmate population problem arising from reform was even more dramatic. Between the low point of 1980 and the high point of 2012, the inmate population of the Federal Bureau of Prisons rose 794 percent. Table 9-1 suggests that most of the increase was a result of the passage of sentencing guidelines in 1987. Between 1978 and 1987 under the indeterminate sentencing law, the prison population rose only 62 percent. However, after sentencing guidelines was passed in 1987, the prison population rose 291 percent. It should also be remembered that rehabilitation was de-emphasized in 1978. The effects of these factors will be examined with respect to recidivism below.

Table 9-1. Prison Population and Sentencing Reform

California				Bureau of Prisons			
	Year	**Count**	**% Change**		**Year**	**Count**	**% Change**
Lowest	1978	21,325		**Lowest**	1980	24,363	
Highest	2006	175,512	+723.0	**Highest**	2012	217,815	+794.0
Determinate Sentencing	1978	21,325		**Indeterminate Sentencing**	1978	29,803	
	1994	126,091	+491.3		1987	48,300	+62.1
Three Strikes	1994	126,091		**Sentencing Guidelines**	1987	48,300	
	2005	170,676	+35.4		2016	189,192	+291.7
Name Change	2005	170,676					
	2016	130,390	-23.6				

Source: National Prisoner Statistics (https://www.bjs.gov/index.cfm?ty=dcdetail&iid=269)

Recidivism after Sentencing Reform

The Office of Research within CDCR is responsible for tracking recidivism. The most recent report is actually quite recent as it was updated in June 2018. The report (CDCR, 2018) provides comparative recidivism data for 11 release cohorts–offenders released in 2002-2003 through 2012-2013. With respect to three-year conviction, return to prison, and arrest rates for offenders released in fiscal year 2002-03 through fiscal year 2012-13; CDCR, 2018: iii), we note the following recidivism data. For all release cohorts except the most recent (2012-2013) the arrest recidivism rate was between 64 percent to 77 percent. This indicates that from 6 to 7 of every 10 offenders released will be rearrested within three years. The conviction rate further shows that generally just under 50 percent (47.3% to 54.3%) of these offenders will be convicted.

These recidivism data are not encouraging. It must be noted that eight of these release cohorts occurred after "rehabilitation" was added to the name of the department. One should have expected significant progress in reducing recidivism. The only good news is for the last release cohort (2012-2013), for which arrest recidivism declined to 66.7 percent and convictions declined to 46.1 percent. Each of these statistics is the lowest across the 11 release cohorts. Perhaps CDCR has turned the corner and it has finally been able to break away from the punishment and custody ideologies to rehabilitation and successful reentry. Only time will tell.

The recidivism data for the Federal Bureau of Prisons are even more problematic. The United States Sentencing Commission has tracked recidivism post implementation of the federal sentencing guidelines. The most recent report (2017) examines 25,431 offenders who were released into the community (either from federal prison or on to probation) in calendar year 2005.

Table 9-2 provides the recidivism data for these federal offenders based on their criminal history category. This report examines 25,431 offenders who were released into the community (either from federal prison or on to probation) in calendar year 2005. Federal sentencing guideline uses criminal history to capture the prior criminality of the offender as part of the sentencing process for the instant offense. An offender's past convictions are assigned one, two, or three points based on the nature of the offense and the sentence and there are six criminal history categories. These point assignments are designed to reflect the seriousness of the prior crime and prior sentence (United States Sentencing Commission, 2017: 6).

Table 9-2 provides data which show a strong connection between criminal history and recidivism. As the criminal history score increases, the recidivism rate increases sharply. Yes, the recidivism rate for category one is a respectable 33.8 percent. However, the offenders with serious prior records of crime reflect a very high probability of recidivating, reaching a high of 80 percent for category 6.

Clearly, federal sentencing reform and the de-emphasis of rehabilitation is correlated with these alarming recidivism data. Federal sentencing guidelines may or may not have eliminated discretion and disparity, while at the same time increasing fairness, equity, and transparency, but said guidelines surely did not have positive effects on recidivism.

Table 9-2. Federal Bureau of Prisons Recidivism Data

Criminal History Category	Number of Offenders	Percent Re-arrested
1	13,581	33.8
2	3,084	54.3
3	3,616	63.3
4	1,996	74.7
5	1,121	77.8
6	1,923	80.1

Source: National Prisoner Statistics (https://www.bjs.gov/index.cfm?ty=dcdetail&iid=269)

The present issue with respect to prisoner reentry has been influenced by external macro level factors like the baby boom phenomenon and its effects on crime rates. But it has also been adversely affected by the advent of determinate sentencing models which have abandoned rehabilitation, have abolished parole, and have thereby exacerbated the smooth and successful reentry of inmates back into society.

Chapter Ten

Prisoner Reentry

Current Status of Prisoner Reentry

In Chapter Nine we argued that while it was time to take stock of the progress which has been made to return offenders to the community with as low a probability of re-offending as possible, we disagreed with the Bureau of Justice Assistance's National Reentry Resource Center in two respects. First, although there have been major sentencing and corrections developments over the past fifteen years, we believe that the 15-year window is entirely too short and fails to account for significant developments prior to 2002 which were the actual forces behind recent developments and the problems the criminal justice system faces today concerning prisoner reentry. Second, although the *Second Chance Act* was important, it was passed during an era which had seen significant changes in sentencing and punishment philosophy. Thus, we believe that a more historical account was needed to understand properly the current situation. Simply, one cannot take a snapshot using an arbitrary point in time and hope to uncover the real driving forces. To the contrary, a longitudinal analysis is required.

We provided a brief account of the history of penology in America. We saw that early prisons were entirely punishment oriented. These so-called penitentiaries were then replaced by reformatories in which rehabilitation became the driving force behind incarceration. We then detailed the swinging of this punishment pendulum in California from rehabilitation to determinate sentencing punishment, then more punishment through a three strikes policy, and then finally a swing back to rehabilitation in 2005. Similarly, the pendulum in the federal system also abandoned rehabilitation in favor of strict punishment through sentencing guidelines and then mandatory minimums for drug offenses which further reinforced punishment ideology.

At this juncture we can now cover the current status of prisoner reentry and propose a model incarceration / reentry system for offenders with co-occurring disorders.

The National Reentry Resource Center's 2017 progress report on prisoner reentry indicated five areas where progress had been made in the ways in which state and local government approaches to reentry and recidivism reduction are fundamentally different today than they were fifteen years ago. These areas are provided below. However, we believe it is our responsibility not just to indicate the progress, but also, to gauge the extent of the progress–a reentry report card essentially.

1. State and Local Priority to Reduce Recidivism

The National Reentry Resource Center indicated that improving reentry and reducing recidivism have become central to the missions of local, state, and federal agencies focused on public safety. The report noted that, since 2012, more than 20 governors have committed to comprehensive policy and practice improvements to achieve statewide reductions in recidivism through initiatives that are supported by Second Chance Act Statewide Adult Recidivism Reduction (SRR) grants. The report also indicated that, in 2016 and 2017, nearly half of U.S. governors cited reentry and reducing recidivism as ongoing efforts or future priorities in State of the State addresses (2017: 4).

Certainly, this is progress. But is it enough progress? We think not. The National Reentry Resource Center data also indicate that about 30 governors have not committed to achieving statewide reductions in recidivism through Second Chance Act grants. This has to change. Perhaps greater technical assistance needs to be provided to the states to help them participate in Second Chance Act initiatives. Similarly, the National Reentry Resource Center data indicated that more than half of the Governors did not sufficiently prioritize prisoner reentry as worthy of mention in State of the State Addresses. Moreover, many of the largest states were in this group: California, Florida, New York, Pennsylvania, and Texas.

2. Constituencies outside Criminal Justice

The National Reentry Resource Center noted that a remarkably diverse set of constituencies outside of the justice system now embraces the goal of helping people who are returning to their communities to succeed after incarceration. The report noted that it is now common for leaders, managers, and front-line staff in government agencies–such as those focused on health and veterans' services, education, and housing–to recognize the stake they have in supporting people under correctional supervision. Similarly, organizations outside of government, such as businesses and faith-based groups, have become increasingly outspoken about the obstacles that people released from prison and jail face (2017: 5).

The National Reentry Resource Center provided extensive evidence to support this conclusion. As of 2017, there were more than 300 Veterans Treatment Courts throughout the country to enable the specific needs of veterans to be considered in release and sentencing decisions. Further, outreach specialists from the Department of Veterans Affairs' Veterans Justice Outreach Program participate in more than 93 percent of Veterans Treatment Court sessions throughout the country (2017: 5).

Employment as part of the reentry process is obviously critical. The National Reentry Resource Center reported that state legislators from across the political spectrum are enacting laws to make it easier for people released from prison and jail to reintegrate into the community. To date, at least 15 states have policies in place to help people obtain state-issued identification after release from prison. Twenty-seven states and more than 150 cities and counties have adopted "ban the box" policies so that people with criminal records are not unnecessarily excluded from the workplace (2017:5).

By account, this second area is a great success. It is crucial for multiple justice system and community agencies to facilitate the reentry progress. Only such a concerted and coordinated effort can hope to facilitate successful reentry.

3. Scientific Advances

The National Reentry Resource Center has correctly noted that the science concerning what works to reduce recidivism has advanced considerably over the last 20 years, and that a rich body of research has emerged. Now, it is commonly understood that each person released from prison has distinct criminogenic risk factors and specific needs. While it may be presumed that the mere existence of a program means that it will benefit a particular person under correctional supervision, in actuality, a particular program will not work when it does not correspond to his or her unique risk and needs. And even when a person needs a particular type of service, such as drug treatment, that service must be delivered according to the program model or it is unlikely to have any impact on a person's behavior. Perhaps most importantly, research has shown that changing the behavior of a person with a medium to high risk of re-offending does not happen through the delivery of a single program or service, or a specific approach to supervision, but rather through a combination of supervision and service strategies that are tailored to the individual risk and needs of that person (2017: 6).

Extensive research has now provided strong evidence that a one size fits all intervention will not work to reduce recidivism. The research issued over the last decade has found that the risk of recidivism, as well as needs related to mental health and substance use treatment, housing, employment, and education, among others, vary significantly from person to person. The data show that treatment, programming, and supervision resources must be deployed in ways that account for a person's specific risk and needs, and that any approach that focuses only on supervision or only on services will have a negligible impact on recidivism (2017: 6).

This third area concerning reentry progress is clearly the most successful. We now have strong research findings to support specific evidence-based strategies to target risks and needs in a strategic fashion designed for specific combinations of risks–especially substance abuse and mental health disorders.

4. Recidivism Tracking

The National Reentry Resource Center indicated that many state and local governments and their community-based partners are applying the latest research to policy, programming, and practice decisions. However, the National Reentry Resource Center indicated that a significant gap still exists between recidivism-reduction science and routine policy and procedure, but states and localities are increasingly translating current recidivism-reduction research into practice (2017: 7).

The National Reentry Resource Center offered the following as evidence of the progress states are making to improve their capacity to measure recidivism. Eleven states monitor re-arrest rates and 15 states monitor re-conviction rates for people released from prison–in addition to tracking re-incarceration rates for people released from prison (2017:7).

Frankly these data are very disappointing and represent the worst progress in any of the five reentry areas identified by the National Reentry Resource Center. Obviously, there is no way for a jurisdiction to gage the success of any intervention efforts whey they are not systematically tracking recidivism. Even if they are taking advantage of the evidence-based initiatives identified by research, the absence of recidivism data renders reentry progress problematic. It is abundantly clear that all jurisdictions must track the following components of recidivism:

- Technical violations of parole or probation;
- Arrest for a new crime;
- Conviction for a new crime;
- Return to prison for a new crime; and
- Time to failure for new arrests.

The National Reentry Resource Center has identified several reasons why the measurement of recidivism is problematic. We reject all of these reasons and suggest that unless and until recidivism tracking is a routine practice of all corrections and parole systems, actual reentry progress will be hidden at best and diminished at worst.

5. Promising Results

The National Reentry Resource Center reported that state and local governments' efforts to apply the latest science are producing results because such progress is based on a commitment to recidivism reduction through the honing of their approaches to improving reentry outcomes. These measurable improvements in recidivism rates are reported in a report entitled "Reducing Recidivism: States Deliver Results" released by The Council of State Governments Justice Center (2017). The report profiles seven states that have seen success across various recidivism measures: re-arrest, re-conviction, re-incarceration, and revocation. Using the most up-to-date data from Arizona, Colorado, Georgia, Michigan, North Carolina, South Carolina, and Texas, the report features data on people under community supervision for a more comprehensive picture of recidivism. For example, (1) in Texas, the number of people revoked to prison from parole declined 33 percent; (2) the number of people returning to Michigan prisons from parole with new convictions dropped 43 percent; and (3) the number of people admitted to North Carolina prisons for probation revocations declined 42 percent (2017: 8).

These results are very encouraging and they indicate the recidivism reduction benefits that can accrue when states avail themselves of evidenced-based strategies. Hopefully, the number of states so doing will increase.

Future Reentry Progress

Before we elaborate on our view of the particulars for successful reentry based on the empirical findings of this evaluation, it is instructive to review the perspective of the National Reentry Resource Center since its mission is to provide up-to-date information about the evolution of prisoner reentry–where we have been, and where we need to go. The National Reentry Resource Center recognizes that the encouraging progress described in its report is still very far from realizing the goal of ensuring that people's transition from prison or jail to the community is safe and successful. To this end, the National Reentry Resource Center offers six functional areas where further progress needs to occur.

1. Align state and local policy with what research demonstrates is effective in reducing recidivism

The National Reentry Resource Center suggests that elected officials and system administrators should push state and local agencies and private service providers to adopt evidence-based practices–such as the use of risk and needs assessments to inform decisions about who receives what programming, services, and supervision. However, the National Reentry Resource Center recognizes that there are existing laws and policies that require people to participate in programs or receive supervision based on the nature of their offense or due to technical factors such as fines and fees that are owed, regardless of whether they need programming or supervision to prevent re-offending. It recommends, therefore, that state and local leaders should identify and revise these existing laws and policies that impede efforts to ground everyday practice in the latest science (2017a: 9).

2. Develop a workforce that understands, embraces, and applies the latest research

The National Reentry Resource Center recognizes that further progress in reentry necessarily involves the countless staff that are involved in corrections. It recommends that changes are needed in the approach that hundreds of thousands of people working for corrections, supervision agencies, and service and treatment providers take to their jobs. Any effort for engaging, motivating, and enhancing the skills and quality of this workforce requires a concerted, long-term effort. It is true that some progress has been made to develop and deliver curricula to new and existing staff, but typically only a fraction of the professionals who would benefit from this training actually receive it. In order to change fundamentally the mindset of the workforce, high level administrators and mid-level managers must commit themselves to overhauling the culture of the organization, which includes steps such as streamlining and automating processes, modifying the approach to personnel reviews and evaluations, and holding accountable those managers who do not embrace and promote these changes (2017a: 9).

3. Improve state and local governments' capacity to collect and analyze data

The National Reentry Resource Center fully realizes that in order to understand whether changes in policy and practice are having their intended impact, elected and appointed officials need recidivism data. It further recognizes that re-incarceration data alone are is insufficient. There is a need for re-conviction and re-arrest data stratified by an offender's risk level, and which is maintained for one-, two-, or three-year follow-up periods. We have commented above that multiple recidivism / outcome measures are crucial for gaging progress in reentry. The usual excuses and caveats about such data must be abandoned and all jurisdictions must improve their recidivism data and analyses with all deliberate speed (2017a: 9).

4. Monitor and assure quality of programs and services

The National Reentry Resource Center's suggestion to monitor and assure the quality of programs and services is extremely important. We specifically adopted a dual component design (outcome evaluation and a process analysis) because it is crucial to have a basis for determining why a supposed evidence-based intervention did not produce the desired recidivism reduction outcome. We fully agree that a key reason for discouraging results is the way in which the intervention was applied. A process analysis or monitoring component provides information concerning how well risk and needs assessments were conducted and even the timing of the assessments–essentially, how well the program was being delivered. This type of quality assurance helps system administrators root out vestiges of practices and programs that research has made clear do not work. It also informs system administrators where gaps in services, skills, training, and policy remain (2017a: 10).

5. Increase investment in effective programs, services, and supervision

The fifth recommendation was seem entirely obvious, but it is crucial nonetheless. Corrections systems cannot afford to continue to deliver services just because that is the way they have always done it. When a probation or parole officer's caseload is impossibly high, it is unrealistic to expect that officer to find the time to provide the type of support and supervision necessary to help a person who is at a medium or high risk of offending to change his or her behaviors. Similarly, a person battling mental illness or addiction is unlikely to get on a path to recovery if he or she does not have access to needed treatment. The National Reentry Resource Center suggests, therefore, that as long as available resources are insufficient to meet existing levels of demand, reductions in recidivism will fall short of what is possible. Investments should occur and resources directed to what the growing body of research indicates are the most promising strategies. Business as usual is a failed policy and must be abandoned.

6. Develop additional knowledge

The last observation from the National Reentry Resource Center is another obvious choice, but it is very important. It argues that, although the research today about "what works" to reduce recidivism is undeniably more robust than it was 15 years ago, there is still much that remains unknown. As an example, it remains unclear what intensity and duration of programming and services is necessary to maximize a person's likelihood of changing criminal thinking and behaviors, and whether it depends on the risk scale or some other more personal, and community-based issues like family cohesion or employment, etc. And, we would argue that we do know sufficiently know how to address the interplay between the substance abuse or mental health components for offenders with co-occurring disorders. Clearly, we need to continue to do research on specific reentry populations and risk assessment scores and the interaction of disorders among offenders who confront multiple risk factors which require multi-faceted interventions (2017a: 10).

Prisoner Reentry for Co-Occurring Disorders

One of our main goals in this book was to provide an evidenced-based model which addresses the incarceration of offenders with co-occurring disorders, and then the implementation of intervention strategies which track towards the transition of these offenders from the institutional setting back into the community. We searched far and wide for such a model. Our search did not produce a workable model that could be applied to both prisons and jails as opposed to just jails, and which detailed both the institutional setting as well as the community reentry setting until we came across the Continuum of Care^{R} model of The GEO Group, Inc. (https://www.geogroup.com/GEOs_Continuum_of_Care). The GEO Continuum of Care is a trademarked approach for enhanced in-custody offender rehabilitation programming, including cognitive behavioral treatment, which is then integrated with post-release support services. The GEO continuum of care utilizes enhanced versions of five components: Assessment, Counseling, Intervention, Transition, and Aftercare. The Geo Group reports that there are more than 30,000 daily participants in evidence-based programming worldwide. In the past ten years, GEO has awarded more than 10,000 GEDs through the company's in-prison academic programs. Over the last decade, approximately 60,000 inmates have achieved completion certificates from a variety of GEO vocational programs. Through GEO's treatment services, over 100,000 inmates have completed substance abuse and therapeutic programs in the last decade. Thus, the GEO continuum of care model has been extensively tested. We provide below the components of the model and then we will apply the model to offenders who have co-occurring disorders.

The GEO Group: Continuum of Care™

We provide below a listing of the GEO Group's continuum of care programming. We did not use any proprietary information–all of the information reported here is publicly available on the company's website. Interested readers should contact the GEO Group for further information (https://www.geogroup.com/GEOs_Continuum_of_Care).

I. In-Custody Programming

- **Academic Programming**
  Use of SMART Board Technology
  Customized Learning Through Individual Education Plans
  Dynamic Grouping
  Technology Based Learning
    - Engaged Learning Model
    - Adult Learner-Centered Approach
    - Technology Integration Zones
    - Collaborative Learning Communities
    - Academic Dorms
    - Technology Based Learning Labs
    - Small Class Sizes
    - Learning and Testing Labs

Differentiated Learning Groups

GEO's Academic Courses Include:

English as a Second Language (ESL)
Literacy
Special Education
GED
Pre-GED

- **Vocational Programming**

GEO's Vocational Programs Include:

Career and Technical Education with Workforce Job Opportunities
National Center for Construction Education and Research (NCCER) Certification
Professional Portfolio Development
Partnerships with Community Employers
Vocational Licensing
On the Job Training Opportunities
Mock Interviews
Project Based Learning
Job Fairs
Nationally Recognized Certification Tracks

GEO's Vocational Licenses Include:

Custodial Maintenance
Barbering
Horticulture
Electrical
Building Trades
Auto Mechanics
Upholstery
Weaving
Heating, Ventilation, and Air Conditioning (HVAC)
Small Engine Repair
Masonry
Plumbing
Culinary Arts
Computer Repair
Carpentry
Welding

- **Cognitive Behavioral Treatment Programs**
    - Motivational Interviewing
    - Cognitive Behavioral Interventions-Substance Abuse (CBI-SA)
    - Success Planning
    - Moral Recognition Therapy (MRT)
    - Cognitive Restructuring
    - Problem Solving
    - Thinking for a Change (T4C)
    - Emotional Regulation
    - Individual Cognitive Behavioral Treatment Sessions (ICBT)
    - Cognitive Self Change

- **Faith-Based Services**
    - Mentoring
    - Modified Therapeutic Community Model
    - Religion Specific Programming
    - Religious Accommodation
    - Pro-Social Modeling
    - Faith and Character Based Housing Units

- **Substance Abuse**
    - Education
    - Residential Drug Abuse Program (RDAP)
    - Gender Responsive Trauma-Informed Care
    - Treatment
    - Living in Balance
    - Alcoholics Anonymous (AA) and Narcotics Anonymous (NA) Programs
    - Cognitive Behavioral Interventions-Substance Abuse (CBI-SA)

II. Post-Release Support Services

Through its Continuum of Care GEO offers a nationwide capability to treat and support culturally unique, vulnerable populations through intensive in-custody, residential, and community-based treatment and support services. The GEO approach offers programs tailored to pretrial, parole, probation, in-custody populations and those involved in immigration proceedings. The programs vary from in-custody and intensive residential treatment, to community-based correctional services and day reporting centers.

- **Transition Planning**
  - Post-Release Residency
  - Identification Needs
  - Financial Needs
  - Employment Opportunities
  - Telephone Contact Information
  - Educational Status
  - Family Contact Information
  - Transportation

- **Case Management**
  - Risk Assessment
  - Cognitive Behavioral Treatment
  - Development of Treatment Plan
  - Advance Skill Practice
  - Periodic Re-assessment and Monitoring
  - Pre-Transitional Planning
  - Treatment Evaluation
  - Clothing

- **Post-Release Support**
  - 24-Hour Call Center
  - Day Reporting Centers
  - Faith-Based Support
  - Case Manager Support

Evidenced-Based Model for Co-Occurring Disorders

Although we are not clinicians, the results of both the statistical analyses of the quantitative outcome variables, and the process analyses of program implementation speak loudly about what should be done with offenders suffering from co-occurring disorders. The results are so clear and convincing that what to do is without much if any dispute. However, we defer to clinicians and therapists to determine how the issue of co-occurring disorders will be approached in terms of choosing screening and assessment tools and then therapeutic interventions. The major results are as follows.

First, in Chapter Five we reported the results of our investigation of the construct validity of the CAAPE for all the subjects in this study (n =170). We reported the following findings. In Table 5-2 for the count of prior arrests we found that the main effects of the CAAPE substance abuse and mental health scores were significant and positive, while the interaction effect was also significant and positive. We noted that this result comports with the concept of co-morbidity–each component of co-occurrence was related to prior criminality. We also showed that the significant and positive interaction effect between the two scores established a reinforcing or synergistic interaction (Afshartous and Preston, 2011). The effect of an increasing mental health score is more pronounced when the substance abuse score also increases and vice versa. Having established the significant interaction effect, we then turned to the main effects of the two variables included in the interaction. These are known as conditional main effects (Afshartous and Preston, 2011). We saw that the mental disorders coefficient (0.200) was much higher than substance abuse (0.044). This signified that the count of arrests increases more for increases in the mental health score than it does for increases in the substance abuse scale score.

Second, in Table 5-3 we saw the results for the analyses of the count of prior conviction charges. It was important to examine this variable because it captures the extent of prior criminality perhaps better than the arrest measure. That is, an offender could be arrested five times and be convicted of five charges, while another offender may also have five prior arrests but was convicted of ten or more charges. Clearly, these two criminal histories do not reflect the same degree of criminality. The Table 5.3 results were as definitive as those in Table 5-2. Table 5-3 indicated like Table 5.2 that there was a significant reinforcing interaction effect of the mental health and substance abuse scores. And again, the conditional main effect of mental health is stronger (0.236) as opposed to substance abuse (0.057).

Third, we also examined the association between the CAAPE scores and post-release recidivism. Table 5-4 provided the logistic regression results for the prediction of recidivism status–whether the subject had any arrests or not after release into the community. The CAAPE measures were significant as found previously. The mental health scores and substance abuse scores had a significant, reinforcing interaction. Likewise, the conditional main effects were also significant and indicated that the strongest predictor of recidivism status was the mental health score (1.087) as compared to substance abuse (0.226). Logistic regression also provided the odds associated with a given predictor. These odds confirm these effects as well. A high mental health score produced a 2.964 greater likelihood of becoming a recidivist as compared to substance abuse, for which the odds were 1.254.

Fourth, Table 5-5 reported the Poisson regression model for the count of arrests after release. These results were very similar to Table 5-4. The measures of prime interest, the CAAPE scores, mirrored the findings from all previous analyses. Mental health disorders and substance abuse showed a reinforcing interaction such that high scores on each dimension was significantly associated with the count of arrests. Likewise, the contingent effects revealed that mental health disorders had a stronger effect (0.831) as compared to substance abuse (0.140). Table 5-6 provided the results for the other quantitative recidivism measure–the extent of the charges for which the subject was convicted upon release into the community. The findings for the CAAPE measures were identical to those reported above. The two dimensions of co-morbidity, mental health disorders and substance abuse, showed a significant reinforcing interaction. The conditional main effects indicate that the mental health disorders factor (1.387) is stronger than substance abuse (0.207).

These consistent results establish the construct validity of the CAAPE. The CAAPE identifies two dimensions of co-occurring disorders: a mental health disorders score and substance abuse score, and these scores are associated with the criminality of the subjects as would be expected.

Major Finding #1

At the time of the entry of the subjects into the county jail, these two dimensions of co-occurring disorders were significantly related to two different measures of prior criminal history–the count of arrests and the count of convictions.

Major Finding #2

At the time of release into the community from the county jail, these co-occurring disorders of these offenders was so chronic that the two CAAPE scores were significantly related to three alternate measures of post-release recidivism: (1) status of recidivist vs. not; (2) count of post-release arrests; and (3) count of post-release convictions.

In addition to the validation results, there are findings available from Chapter 7 where we investigated the situation for the experimental group alone to see why the program failed to produce the desired recidivism reduction. There were three notable findings to be considered in a reentry model.

First, Table 7-9 showed a Poisson regression of the number of charges for which the recidivist was convicted after reentering the community. The total LS/CMI score across Section 1 was a significant predictor of convictions. The higher the total score the more convictions that occurred.

Likewise, Table 7.10 showed a Poisson regression model using the eight subscales of Section 1. It was highly important that all of these subscales had significant coefficients, thus indicating they were significant predictors of the count of convictions. These coefficients suggested that the experimental group subjects who had high scores on these subscales posed significantly increased risk of recidivism. The reentry program did not address these client issues sufficiently to prevent the recidivism that would be a natural consequence of these risk factors.

Second, in addition to these LS/CMI effects, we also found significant co-occurring disorder effects. In Table 7-11,we saw that the total mental health score of the CAAPE had a significant and positive effect on convictions.

Third, Tables 7-12 and 7-13 examined specific factors contained in the overall substance abuse score and the mental health score. Table 7-12 indicated that subjects with a marijuana abuse profile had a significant and positive effect on convictions. However, alcohol and stimulant abusers also had significant negative effects on convictions. Table 7-13 presented very important findings because six of the nine disorder types had significant effects on recidivism–some were positive and some were negative. There were four CAAPE mental disorders that had significant and positive consequences for recidivism: PTSD, obsessive/compulsive, psychosis, and anti-social personality. Experimental group subjects with these disorders accumulated a greater number of post-release recidivism. Alternatively, there were two CAAPE disorders, major depressive and manic, that were significantly associated with a lower count of post-release convictions.

All these multi-variate results across the LS/CMI and CAAPE for experimental group subjects are crucially important to corrections administrators, clinicians, and community reentry service organizations. These factors represent serious underlying disorders that must be remediated in order to reduce the risk of recidivism.

Major Finding #3

Offenders with high scores on one or more of the LS/CMI subscales have serious risks / needs that must be addressed prior to reentry back into the community. Thus, very focused transition planning must be accomplished before release into the community. And, there needs to be continuity of care after release to ensure that the needs are being addressed in order to avoid the high probability of recidivism.

Major Finding #4

There are offenders with high scores on dimension of both substance abuse and mental health disorders that are at increased risk for recidivism. These substance abuse issues must be addressed while incarcerated through appropriate interventions and therapy. Further, these disorders can be so chronic that plans need to be formulated for continuing to address these disorders after release back into the community.

Co-Occurring Disorders: Incarceration through Reentry

Based on these four major findings, we have provided below an outline of the components necessary to identify, treat, and release offenders with co-occurring disorders back into society.

During the incarceration period, we see three major components. First, screening for substance abuse and mental health disorders should take place with every inmate during the intake process. Mandatory screening will ensure that inmates are placed in appropriate settings within the institution but may also establish the need for clinical assessment to diagnose more specifically and clearly the presence of co-occurring disorders. Screening is easily implemented by correctional facilities, as most instruments do not require trained or licensed clinicians to conduct the instruments (see Chapter 3: Figures 3-1, 3-2, 3-3).

Second, however, our preference is that all inmates should be assessed at intake. Early assessment would provide faster access to support and resources inside the facility. It would also allow correctional staff to develop a plan tailored to the individual before any time is lost with unnecessary or incorrect programming. This is crucial in county jails where inmates generally serve up to two or two and one-half years of prison time. Also, many inmates are unwilling to participate in multiple interviews or tests, thus reducing the number of sessions to just the assessment would ensure a better rapport but could also increase the likelihood of truthful answers. Further, screening instruments may lead to false negatives, where individuals who are suffering from either mental health or substance use disorders may be missed and not receive an assessment that would later inform correctional agents of the individuals' true diagnosis. Skipping directly to the assessment would eliminate the possibility of delayed assessment or no assessment at all. We have identified the assessment instruments in Chapter 3: Figures 3-4, 3-5, 3-6.

Third, treatment for the co-occurring disorders is the major component during the incarceration stage. We have borrowed the approach of the

GEO Group because it seems comprehensive and targets the specific disorders with focused interventions. Naturally, clinicians are free to choose their own therapeutic interventions. As noted, it is crucial for the treatment of co-occurring disorders to commence as quickly as possible in county jails and it is likely that treatment will necessarily have to continue after release. We have also identified the need for academic and vocational programs to reduce the recidivism risk of these factors.

The second major component in our model is reentry planning. In this research we found that the reentry/discharge planning suffered from two defects. First, the planning occurred too close to the time of release to be effective. There was just not sufficient time to coordinate the community resources that would be required to address the risks and needs of the offenders. Second, we also found that the services identified were too generic and did not appear to be calibrated to the risks that were identified by the LS/CMI. Both of these defects need to be eliminated if offender reentry has any chance at all of being successful.

Thus, reentry planning involves the following activities. First, the risks and needs of each specific offender must be scored via the LS/CMI or a comparable instrument. The LS/CMI includes eight major subscales which cover important risks and the identification of crucial everyday services and needs. Second, after risk and needs assessment is accomplished, reentry planning should formalize a treatment plan for the individual offender. Most important, reentry planning should identify and make arrangements with community-based agencies who will provide the specific treatments and services.

The third major component of our proposed model is post-release support. We envision this as a heavy case management function to assure that reentry is occurring in accord with the discharge plan and the offender is embracing the plan. Thus, case management must ensure continual communication with the offender personally and with his family and work location. The major activity of the case management is to conduct continual monitoring of the offender after release. Is he receiving the required treatment as identified by his risk scores? Is he receiving the required services as identified by his needs assessment? Strong case management upon release into the community and the continual monitoring of the offender will ensure the greatest chances for successful reentry.

Evidence-Based Reentry

I. Incarceration

A. Intake Screening

B. Assessment

C. Treatment

1. Substance Abuse [The GEO Group's Continuum of Care[R]]

Education
Residential Drug Abuse Program (RDAP)
Gender Responsive Trauma-Informed Care
Treatment
Living in Balance
Alcoholics Anonymous (AA) and Narcotics Anonymous (NA) Programs
Cognitive Behavioral Interventions-Substance Abuse (CBI-SA)

2. Mental Health Disorders [The GEO Group's Continuum of Care[R]]

Cognitive Behavioral Treatment Programs
Motivational Interviewing
Cognitive Behavioral Interventions-Substance Abuse (CBI-SA)
Success Planning
Moral Recognition Therapy (MRT)
Cognitive Restructuring
Problem Solving
Thinking for a Change (T4C)
Emotional Regulation
Individual Cognitive Behavioral Treatment Sessions (ICBT)
Cognitive Self Change

3. Academic Programs

4. Vocational Programs

II. Reentry Planning

A. Risk and Needs Assessment

1. LS/CMI [or the equivalent]

Criminal History
Education/Employment
Family/Marital
Leisure/Recreation
Companions

Alcohol/Drugs
Pro Crime Attitude
Anti-Social Pattern

2. Reentry Treatment Plan

Identification of specific risks and needs
Identification of community resources

III. Post-Release Support

A. Case Management

1. Communication

Offender contact information
Family contact information
Offender work contact information

2. Monitoring

Periodic assessment of Treatment
Work
Risks
Needs

CHAPTER ELEVEN

SUMMARY

This book is an outgrowth of a partnership between the School of Criminology and Justice Studies, University of Massachusetts Lowell, and the Essex County, Massachusetts, Sheriff's Department. Essex County applied for funding through the Bureau of Justice Assistance's Second Chance Act Reentry Program for Adult Offenders with Co-Occurring Substance Abuse and Mental Health Disorders (solicitation: BJA-2014-3773). The Essex County proposal was funded in 2014 for a two-year period (BJA grant #: 2014-RW-BX-0001). The BJA solicitation reflected a growing concern with prisoner reentry, especially for offenders with co-occurring disorders. The BJA solicitation indicated the following two manifold principles.

First, the Reentry Program for Adult Offenders with Co-Occurring Substance Abuse and Mental Health Disorders is designed to improve outcomes for adults with co-occurring substance abuse and mental health disorders through the screening and assessment of incarcerated individuals, availability of some pre-release programming, leading to the provision of appropriate evidence-based services and treatment after incarceration (BJA: p. 4).

Second, BJA recognized that a significant number of individuals who are incarcerated and returning to the community have chronic substance abuse and mental health disorders and are in need of treatment in order to successfully complete their supervision, reduce recidivism, and promote public safety. The coordination of substance abuse and mental health treatment with correctional planning can encourage participation in treatment and can help treatment providers incorporate correctional requirements as treatment goals (BJA: p.5).

Our role in the grant was to conduct an evaluation using a rigorous experimental design of Essex County's program. The evaluation function is mandated by the Second Chance Act. That is, the Act requires an evaluation of all Second Chance Act programs by an outside, objective evaluator so that evidenced-based policies and practices will emerge from Second Chance Act grants, and thus, serve public policy in a definitive manner because they are supported by empirical findings that are rigorous and defensible.

As we began work on the project and acquainted ourselves with the literature on prisoner reentry, clinical assessments, and treatment approaches, we soon realized that there were disparate audiences, discipline specific journals, and even technical assistance reports that were published. We came to believe that there were scarce publications that brought together the extant literature, while at the same time, also reported crucial empirical findings such as those in the present work. One of our primary concerns was that, while many publications addressed the contemporary state of prisoner reentry and the problem surrounding the release of offenders with co-occurring disorders, much of this literature lacked historical context. Thus, the present work has attempted to remedy this deficiency and the work was organized to achieve this goal.

In Chapter One we employed a historical perspective. We showed that although serious concern over prisoner reentry did not arise and take hold until 1999, the seeds of the reentry problem were established long before then and available data clearly indicated a reentry problem that likely would not only continue, but also, would increase significantly. We showed that one of the significant factors behind the reentry problem was the "baby boom" phenomenon. The so-called baby boom began in 1945 and lasted until 1964. More babies were born in 1946 than ever before–3.4 million, 20 percent more than in 1945. In 1947, another 3.8 million babies were born; 3.9 million were born in 1952; and more than 4 million were born every year from 1954 until 1964, when the boom finally tapered off. By then, there were 76.4 million "baby boomers" in the United States. They made up almost 40 percent of the nation's population.

We reviewed research which illustrated that the baby boom phenomenon did have an effect on increased crime rates, and concomitantly, would have similar effects on incarceration rates, the size of the prison population, and the volume of inmates being released back into society. We provided data in several charts which indicated a clear trend which framed the reentry issue over time. The rate at which criminals were imprisoned started at 131 per 100,000 in 1978 and rose each and every year, reaching its peak of 506 per 100,000 in 2008. That is 31 consecutive years of increased use of prison as a form of punishment. From 2009 to 2016 the imprisonment rate declined to a low of 450 in 2016, a rate which is still over 3.5 times higher than in 1978. The effect of these rising imprisonment rates on the size of the prison population was clearly evident. In 1978, the prison population was 307,276 inmates. The prison population increased unabated from 1978 to 2010 at which point there were 1,613,083 inmates in prison. This constituted a 425 percent increase in the prison population. The prison population declined slightly between 2011 and 2016 and reached a low of 1,505,396 in 2016.

Thus, the combined effects of rising crime rates and increased imprisonment lead to a dramatic rise in the prison population. The effect on the inmate reentry issue starts to become clear. The concerns raised by scholars takes on even greater significance when recent reentry data are examined. The sheer size of the reentry population warrants increased attention. In 2010, 708,677 inmates were released back to their communities (Guerino, Harrison, and Sabol, 2010), and in 2011, 688,384 offenders, approximately 1,885 individuals per day, were released from state or federal custody (Carson and Sobel, 2012). But we could be even more definitive concerning the inmate release data. Our data indicated that 142,665 inmates were released back into society in 1978–about 390 inmates per day. From 1978 to 2008 the number of inmates released from state and federal prisons increased annually and reached a peak of 735,651 inmates released–a 415 percent increase in the reentry population.

Chapter One also reviewed the literature on recidivism to document the problem that must be confronted when considering the reentry of inmates back into society. Fortunately for us, there was a very recent study from the Bureau of Justice Statistics (BJS) which provided definitive data on post-release recidivism. Alper and Durose (2018) examined the post-release offending patterns of former prisoners and their involvement in criminal activity both within and outside of the state where they were imprisoned. The study employed a very rigorous research design with sophisticated sampling to study 67,966 prisoners who were randomly sampled to represent the 401,288 state prisoners released in 2005 in 30 states. The sample was representative of the 30 states, both individually and collectively. In 2005, these 30 states were responsible for 77 percent of all persons released from state prisons nationwide. The findings were highly pertinent to the present investigation because they provided longitudinal data on post-release recidivism across all the major demographic characteristics of released prisoners and a very long, nine-year follow-up period.

The findings with regard to the percentage of released inmates who recidivated across the nine-year period were worthy of serious consideration in a number of respects.

First, by the end of the nine years, 83.4 percent of the cases had recidivated at least once. Thus, a prison sentence to punish these criminals and exercise specific deterrence had failed to deter future criminality for 8.3 out of every 10 inmates.

Second, the study also provided a year by year accounting of the recidivism. These results pointed to the serious problem surrounding community reentry. That is, 43.9 percent of the sample had been rearrested during the first year of release from prison. In year two, another 17.8 percent had been rearrested which brought the cumulative recidivism total to 60.1 percent. Thus, six out of 10 of the cases had become criminals once again by the end of the second year. This figure rose to 68.4 percent by the end of year three.

Third, Alper and Durose also provided nine-year recidivism data across the major demographic characteristics. Usually in criminological research these data, whether it be the prevalence or incidence of crime, or even the severity, vary considerably across these factors. The researcher has to take into account the differential criminogenic influences underlying the different factors. Simply, research shows very different crime patters for males v. females, across younger age groups v. older, and across race/ethnicity categories. Not this time, however. The results were remarkably consistent. Females only trailed males by less than 8 percent. Similarly, across race/ethnicity categories, the highest recidivism percent for African Americans (86.9%) was only greater than the lowest score for Asians, Native Hawaiians, and other Pacific Islanders (79.4%) by 7.5 percent. Usually, age categories show very disparate differences because crime varies strongly by age. But the findings indicated that the most crime prone age group of age 24 or younger, only differed by from 3 to 5 percent for all other ages except for the oldest category of age 40 or older for which the difference is 13.6 percent. Clearly, the recidivism data across these demographic factors strongly indicated that all released prisoners, regardless of sex, age, or race/ethnicity exhibit substantial and consistent recidivism over time.

Fourth, Alper and Durose also provided data concerning the incidence or extent of post-release recidivism across the nine-year period following the release back into the community. Overall, these criminals committed a total of 1,994,000 offenses during the nine years. Further, although over 40 percent were committed in the first three years after release, 31 percent were committed in years four through six, while 28.6 percent were committed in years seven through nine. Thus, sixty percent of these recidivist crimes occurred across a lengthy time span thus indicating that prior punishment was a minor deterrent, and that reentry was an abysmal failure.

Overall therefore, a very recent BJS study established the following. Among, 1,000 prisoners returned to the community, 830 were rearrested. A substantial percentage of recidivism was evident across both sexes and across all age groups and race/ethnicity categories. The criminality of these recidivists was extensive as almost 2,000,000 (1,994,000) arrests were recorded across the nine-year follow-up period.

Chapter Two reviewed the research literature concerning three major risk factors associated with criminal behavior. These factors were: (1) substance use disorders; (2) mental illness disorders: and (3) the co-occurrence of both of these two risk factors. There was substantial literature on the first two risk factors, but comparatively less on co-occurring disorders. For all three risk factors, the prevalence of these phenomena was found to be considerably higher among criminals than is the case among the general public.

We reported extensive national data from the *National Survey on Drug Use and Health* from the Center for Behavioral Health Statistics and Quality, Substance Abuse and Mental Health Services Administration (SAMHSA, 2015). These data indicated that among persons 12 years old and older, 21.5 million people, or 8.1 percent, were classified as having a substance use disorder (SUD). The results further showed that 17 million people (6.4%) had an alcohol use disorder, while 7.1 million people (2.6%) had an illicit drug use disorder.

However, we also cautioned that these percentage statistics are an undercount because children aged 12 through 17 are included in the data. If data were reported only for adults the percentages would be much higher. The criminal justice context of substance use disorders is extensive among criminals.

First, substantial proportions of offenders have diagnosed substance abuse issues. The most recent data from the Center for Substance Abuse (CASA) showed that of the 2.3 million adults behind bars, 1.9 million (83%) were substance involved–an increase from the 80 percent in 1996. CASA's second study also indicated that the substance abuse problem among inmates had also increased across all correctional venues: 84.8 percent of all inmates (1.9 million) were substance involved, 86.2 percent of federal inmates (200,00), 84.6 percent of state inmates (1.1 million) and 84.7 percent of local jail inmates (600,000). CASA's data also found that and almost two-thirds (64.5 percent) met the medical DSM-IV criteria for an alcohol or other drug use disorder.

Second, in all the studies reviewed, significant percentages of inmates, regardless of whether they met the DSM-IV medical criteria for alcohol and other drug abuse and addiction, were substance involved–that is, they were under the influence of alcohol or other drugs at the time of their offense, stole money to buy drugs, were substance abusers, violated alcohol or drug laws, or share some combination of these characteristics.

The two CASA studies were corroborated by two Bureau of Justice Statistics reports Karberg and James (2005, widely cited) found that 50 percent of jail inmates in 2002 were substance abusers. They also noted (like CASA) that 80 percent of jail inmates were substance involved and 40 percent had a substance use disorder. Similarly, Mumula and Karberg (2006) found that 45 percent of federal inmates and 53 percent of state inmates were substance abusers.

Third, many criminals used drugs proximal to the time of their offenses or were under the influence of drugs at the time they were arrested.

The literature indicated that the prevalence estimates of mental health disorders are considerably lower than substance use disorders. The Substance Abuse and Mental Health Services Administration study reported that in 2014, 43.6 million people, 18.1 percent of the general population, had a diagnosed mental illness. The prevalence drops to 4.1 percent (9.8 million people) for the prevalence of a serious mental illness (SAMHSA, 2015). In the criminal justice system studies have generally indicated that about 16 percent of inmates have a diagnosed mental illness problem. On the high end, James and Gaze (2006) found that more 54 percent of all prison and jail inmates had a mental health problem, including 56 percent of state prisoners, 45 percent of federal prisoners, and 64 percent of jail inmates.

The Substance Abuse and Mental Health Services Administration reported that co-occurring disorders are very rare. According to the study, an estimated 7.9 million people, or just 3.3 percent of the general population has a diagnosed co-occurring disorder (SAMSHA, 2015).

Our principal concern in Chapter Two was to summarize the results concerning the extent of co-occurring disorders among justice-involved persons. Despite the fact that numerous observers point out the importance of investigating co-occurring disorders, and that reentry is compromised because of these disorders, there is paucity of definitive research. There were few studies which report the actual prevalence of co-occurring disorders. There were even fewer studies that reported useable percentages. Realistically, there were only two studies (James and Gaze, 2006; Blandford and Osher, 2013) which provided adequate data on the underlying percentages of substance abuse disorders and mental illness disorders. These studies were in general agreement that co-occurring disorders affect between 7 percent and 12 percent of inmates across all the corrections venues.

Suffice it to say, therefore, that a conservative estimate is that incarcerated offenders suffer from co-occurring disorders from two to four times as often as the general public. We suspect that this range is an underestimate but only further research will facilitate the resolution of the exact situation. We suspect that the ratio is much higher but there are just insufficient data. One major reason for the lack of competent data is that we also suspect that the screening and assessment of co-occurring disorders is not happening in correctional settings to the extent that it should.

Chapter Three addressed the screening and assessment for substance abuse, mental illness, and co-occurring disorders. We provided expert commentary on the differences between screening and assessment. We also provided information concerning the importance of these processes and the barriers to the effective use of screening and assessment in correctional settings.

The literature indicated, of course, that screening is just the first step in providing a proper pathway toward recovery. Ideally, after being screened, individuals identified as suffering from co-occurring disorders will be further assessed via proper assessment tools. Thus, screening alone really is not sufficient and the assessment of inmates to fully diagnose and understand the extent of their issues is preferred.

To reduce recidivism, but also to aid in the recovery of inmates, the tools need to be utilized to guide the discharge plan and reentry services. They cannot merely be a tool used to designate a living space for inmates. Screening and assessment should be done on a continuous basis to verify that the needs of the inmates are being met and that the diagnoses are, in fact, correct. At a minimum, assessment should occur at intake, and before release.

We also briefly reviewed a few promising treatment programs for co-occurring disorders. Programs like cognitive behavioral therapy and modified treatment communities are reflected in a growing body of research as best practices for co-occurring disorders.

Chapter Four laid out the research design that we used in the evaluation of the Essex County program. We indicated that the best research design would involve two components. First, an outcome evaluation would document the extent to which ECSD's COD program achieved the desired effects. In the present context, this concerns the extent to which the COD program did in fact result in: (1) evidence-based screening of CODs: (2) identification and provision of community reentry services; and (3) lower recidivism. Second, we showed that the evaluation should also include a process evaluation. Process analyses are often neglected in evaluation research studies. This is unfortunate because this type of evaluation research can generate findings that provide important feedback concerning service delivery itself. The present process analysis monitored program activities, but instead of inmate reentry/recidivism being the ultimate outcome measure, the process evaluation focused on various measures of program participation and fidelity and measured the consistency and successful implementation of the program, separate and apart from outcomes.

Thus, the two components of the evaluation functioned together to ensure the ability of the evaluation to identify best practices. The usual outcome analyses are of course significant. After all, the ultimate purpose of the COD Program was to deliver more effective treatment to inmates thus leading to reduced recidivism. Clearly, however, an evaluation should not focus disproportionately, and certainly not exclusively, on outcome measures per se, and neglect program implementation features. By ignoring a process analysis, the capacity of the evaluation to yield information is diminished concerning how and why ECSD might have been able to achieve comparatively better success rates than it has in the past. The design is superior to the usual outcome evaluation and provides much greater opportunity for achieving an outcome assessment while at the same time providing important contextual data concerning program participation and delivery.

Chapter Five provided the results of our effort to validate the assessment instrument used in the program. Our goal in Chapter Five was to add to a growing body of research concerning the relationship between co-occurring disorders and criminal behavior by investigating the construct validity of the CAAPE. The results of rigorous multi-variate models indicated that the CAAPE appears to have construct validity because it captured two principal components of co-morbidity: mental health disorders and substance abuse. The findings with respect to five different criminal history measures were definitive.

First, the CAAPE measures were significant, mutually reinforcing factors of criminal behavior. Second, the mental disorders component was stronger than the effect of substance abuse. Third, the CAAPE measures remained significant after controlling for many other variables that are usually related to criminal behavior and often have very strong effects in their own right. Here, however, the CAAPE measures were stronger and had significant effects.

These results indicate that further research is warranted to provide additional validation data for the CAAPE. Such research should cross-validate the CAAPE with justice-involved persons with other co-occurring disorder screening instruments. It would also be advisable to investigate the comparative validity of the CAAPE with varying samples of offenders–those in jails and those in state prison serving longer sentences.

The results reported here nevertheless suggested a pressing need to assess offenders upon entry to correctional facilities and then again before release. The CAAPE measures were significantly related to prior criminal record and it is likely that co-morbidity was an important criminogenic factor. Moreover, because co-morbidity was also related to post-release recidivism, it is also likely that co-morbidity represents a chronic condition which drives criminality even after incarceration ends if it is not properly treated. Clinicians would be wise to assess all inmates with tools such as the CAAPE so that co-occurring disorders can be identified and focused treatment undertaken. This is the case because both institutional adjustment and future recidivism upon community reentry seem clearly connected causally.

Chapter Six focused on the outcome component of the evaluation. It provided the results for the comparison of the recidivism between the experimental and control groups. Given that a variety of reentry services were provided to the experimental group, it would certainly be expected that the experimental group would exhibit a significantly lower percentage of recidivists, regardless of the particular way in which recidivism was measured.

We analyzed bi-variate cross-tabulations across four measures of recidivism. We also analyzed the type of recidivism offense. We compared the mean number of recidivism offenses. The findings for all these the descriptive analyses were unequivocal. Across five categorical variables and four quantitative variables of recidivism, none of the comparisons revealed significant findings. For all measures, the experimental and control groups had statistically equivalent recidivism data. These findings indicated that the program failed to reduce recidivism for subjects in the experimental group despite having received reentry services as opposed to the control group who did not receive any community-based services at all.

We recognized that it is unwise to develop strong conclusions using only basic descriptive analyses. While such descriptive analyses are essential to capture the distributional parameters of the recidivism dependent variable, descriptive analyses do not permit examination of the dependent variable while controlling for other predictor variables that could be influencing the recidivism criterion measures. This can only be accomplished with multi-variate models. In the present case, we had both dichotomous and quantitative measures of recidivism. Thus, we analyzed the data using rigorous modeling techniques such as logistic regression, Poisson regression, and ordinary least squares regression.

We conducted logistic regression models for the four dichotomous recidivism measures to determine whether the program variable (experimental vs. control) had a significant effect on the alternate measures of recidivism status. The models also included the effects of three other blocks of variables (demographic, criminal history, and co-occurring disorder scores) as covariates. The results for all four models were unequivocal–the program did not result in lower recidivism for the experimental group. By virtue of the sign of the coefficient for the program variable, the experimental group was more likely to be an overall recidivist and a technical violator, while the control group was more likely to be arrested or convicted. But, none of these coefficients were significant.

The analyses for the four quantitative measures of recidivism, like the binary variables reported above, were also unequivocal. The program did not produce diminished recidivism when measured quantitatively. The program variable was not significant in any of the four analyses. Although not significant, the coefficients do indicate some interesting effects. The experimental group was more likely to accumulate a higher number of arrests, but a fewer number of convictions. Also, the experimental group had a lower recidivism offense scale score, but it also had a faster time to failure.

Further, the multi-variate models concerning both the binary recidivism status variables and the quantitative recidivism counts indicated that only familiar criminological and demographic variables were significantly related to recidivism, while program membership was not. All of these rigorous statistical techniques failed to uncover any evidence that the reentry services provided to the experimental group made any difference whatsoever in terms of recidivism.

In Chapter Seven, because none of the group comparison analyses indicated that the program made a significant difference with respect to a multiple of measures of recidivism, we then focused on the experimental group itself and examined descriptive data and multi-variate models comparing the experimental group recidivists to the experimental group non-recidivists. These analyses identified possible reasons why more than 50 percent of the experimental group recidivated.

The descriptive data indicated that the overall LS/CMI score and the eight subscales were higher for the experimental group recidivists, thus indicating a clinical diagnosis of greater problems than the experimental group subjects who did not recidivate. Further, the overall score, family/marital subscale and Pro Crime Attitude subscale were significantly higher for the recidivists. Likewise, the descriptive data showed very clearly that the recidivist subset had greater risk of recidivism for all the prior criminal history risk factors. Recidivists had higher prior arrests, had longer time served, and were younger. Most important, the experimental recidivists had a significantly higher number of prior convictions, which we have seen in previous analyses was definitively related to recidivism in this evaluation for all cases. The experimental recidivists had higher CAAPE scores for all five measures reflective of co-occurring disorders although these differences were not significant. However, only one of the CAAPE drugs of abuse, cocaine, showed a significant difference and this coefficient indicated that the experimental group had a significantly higher mean level of involvement with cocaine prior to the current incarceration.

The multi-variate models of recidivism for the experimental group analyses did reveal some important results. The total LS/CMI score across Section 1 was a significant predictor of convictions. The higher the total score, the more convictions that occurred. Likewise, for the eight subscales of the LS/CMI Section 1, four of these coefficients were significant predictors of the count of convictions. The criminal history, education/employment, pro-crime attitudes, and anti-social patterns had significant, positive effects on convictions. These coefficients suggest that the experimental group subjects who had high scores on these four subscales posed significantly increased risk of recidivism.

Thus, the reentry program did not address these client issues sufficiently to prevent the recidivism that would be a natural consequence of these risk factors.

In addition to the identification of LS/CMI effects, we also found significant co-occurring disorder factors. The total mental health score of the CAAPE had a significant and positive effect on convictions as did a marijuana abuse profile. However, alcohol and stimulant abusers had significant negative effects on convictions. We also uncovered very important findings concerning the types of mental health disorders–five of the nine disorder types had significant effects on recidivism–some were positive and some were negative. There were three CAAPE mental disorders that had significant and positive consequences for recidivism: PTSD, obsessive/compulsive, and anti-social personality. Experimental group subjects with these disorders accumulated a greater number of post-release recidivism. Alternatively, there were two CAAPE disorders, major depressive and manic, that were significantly associated with a lower count of post-release convictions.

These multi-variate results across the LS/CMI and CAAPE scores are important to corrections administrators, clinicians, and community reentry service organizations. These factors represent serious underlying disorders that must be remediated in order to reduce the risk of recidivism. In the present case, these risks as identified via both the LS/CMI scores and specific CAAPE indicators did not seem to elicit targeted and highly specific reentry services to remediate these recidivism factors.

Chapter Eight focused on the process analysis and was a natural extension of Chapters Six and Seven. Overall, the process analysis was a valuable component in this research. Through the day-to-day monitoring of all aspects of the program, the process analysis generated the following major findings.

The Essex County Reentry Program for Adult Offenders with Co-Occurring Disorders was a diligent and committed effort to address the reentry needs and recidivism risks of an experimental group of subjects who received reentry services. The program was staffed by dedicated professionals, both within and without the institution. Unfortunately, the success of the program was likely diminished by several factors that must be avoided in future reentry programs.

First, the planning stage was entirely too long and necessarily delayed important aspects of the program. In fact, the planning stage was so long that implementation activities did not occur until ten months after the grant started.

Second, this delay lead to a series of other delays which compromised the potential of the program to render significant effects on the recidivism outcome.

The scoring matrix for the CAAPE was not developed early enough in the planning stage which caused ripple effects throughout the implementation stage. Because the scoring matrix was not developed and authorized for program use until 21 September 2015, the determination of case eligibility and then random assignment to the experimental and control groups was severely delayed. The first CAAPE was administered on 21 September 2015, and the last was administered on 9 December 2015. Thus, the composition of the two experimental groups was not finalized until late December 2015.

Following random assignment to the experimental group and control group, the experimental group subjects had to be assessed via the LS/CMI, which in concert with the scores from the CAAPE, became the basis for the Discharge Plan that would guide the reentry process. In turn the discharge plan informed the service goals that were targeted for reentry services. Because of the earlier delays, both of these processes had to occur quite quickly over a relatively short period of time.

The cumulative effect of all the delays can be best evidenced with respect to the release dates for the experimental group. The earliest release occurred on 1 November 2015, while the latest happened on 21 April 2016 (the dates were virtually the same for the control group). The delayed release dates thus reduced the time that subjects would be at risk in the community for the measurement of recidivism. Thus, the recidivism rates in this program might be even higher if all cases had a one-year follow-up period.

Third, the community-based services that were derived from the LS/CMI and CAAPE risk assessment tools and then the discharge plans, appeared to be more generic service goals rather than individual-specific service goals reflective of the serious underlying disorders present in many of the experimental subjects. We found little evidence that the co-occurring disorders of the experimental group were addressed in any clinically sufficient fashion.

In Chapter Nine we took exception to two recent claims from the National Reentry Resource Center. The first claim was that one of the most significant developments in criminal justice policy over the past 15 years has been a fundamental shift in thinking about the primary purpose of prisons and jails. The second claim was that although no single event is associated with this change in philosophy, a key milestone stands out. Late in 2004, Congress set to work on the Second Chance Act, which the House and Senate later passed with overwhelming bipartisan support.

While we agree, that there have been major sentencing and corrections developments over the past fifteen years, we believe that the 15-year window is entirely too short and fails to account for significant developments prior to 2002 which were the actual forces behind recent developments and the problems the criminal justice system faces today concerning prisoner reentry. What factors led to a shift in thinking about the primary purpose of prisons and jails? Did these factors emerge at a specific juncture, or were these factors the result of long-term developments? We believe that a more historical account is needed to understand properly the current situation. Simply, one cannot take a snapshot using an arbitrary point in time and hope to uncover the real driving forces. To the contrary, a longitudinal analysis is required. Likewise, the identification of the *Second Chance Act* is also shortsighted. What were the driving forces behind the Act? Why did Congress entertain passage of this Act in 2004, and not for example, in 1994 or 1998 or any particular year for that matter? We believe once again that a much longer-range view is needed to grasp the dynamics of the environment in which the Act was passed. Consequently, Chapter Nine evolved into an analysis of important historical developments in penology which are crucial for an understanding the current issues–especially reentry.

We provided a historical account of what we called the punishment pendulum. We showed that the philosophy concerning the incarceration of criminals did in fact swing between punishment and rehabilitation from the outset of corrections in America. In particular, we showed that sentencing developments in both California and the federal system in the 1970s and 1980s had a far greater impact on the problem of contemporary prisoner reentry than any recent developments.

The sentencing reforms in California and at the federal level came during a period of rising crime rates and increasing incarceration rates as detailed in Chapter One. This was perhaps not the best time to abandon rehabilitation. Table 9-1 captures the relationship between the sentencing reforms and the changes in the inmate population in California and the Bureau of Prisons.

In California, the prison population increased 723 percent from 1978 to 2006. During this period several reforms were instituted. First, rehabilitation was abandoned and determinate sentencing was implemented in 1978. Between 1978 and 1994, when Three Strikes was passed, the prison population increased 491 percent. Second, despite this startling increase in the prison population as of 1994, California passed Three Strikes and the inmate population rose another 35 percent as of 2005. Finally, in 2005 California changed the name and the focus of the corrections department to the California Department of Correction and Rehabilitation.

At the federal level, the inmate population problem arising from reform was even more dramatic. Between the low point of 1980 and the high point of 2012, the inmate population of the Federal Bureau of Prisons rose 794 percent. The data suggested that most of the increase was a result of the passage of sentencing guidelines in 1987. Between 1978 and 1987 under the indeterminate sentencing law, the prison population rose only 62 percent. However, after sentencing guidelines was passed in 1987, the prison population rose 291 percent. It should also be remembered that rehabilitation was de-emphasized in 1978. The effects of these factors were examined with respect to recidivism.

We analyzed data from the Office of Research within CDCR. The CDCR data provided comparative recidivism data for 11 release cohorts–offenders released in 2002-2003 through 2012-2013. With respect to three-year conviction, return to prison, and arrest rates for offenders released in fiscal year 2002-03 through fiscal year 2012-13; we noted the following recidivism data. For all release cohorts except the most recent (2012-2013) the arrest recidivism rate was between 64 percent to 77 percent. This indicates that from 6 to 7 of every 10 offenders released will be rearrested within three years. The conviction rate further shows that generally just under 50 percent (47.3% to 54.3%) of these offenders will be convicted.

These recidivism data are not encouraging. It must be noted that eight of these release cohorts occurred after "rehabilitation" was added to the name of the department. One should have expected significant progress in reducing recidivism. The only good news is for the last release cohort (2012-2013) for which arrest recidivism declined to 66.7 percent and convictions declined to 46.1 percent. Each of these statistics is the lowest across the 11 release cohorts. Perhaps CDCR has turned the corner and it has finally been able to break away from the punishment and custody ideologies to rehabilitation and successful reentry. Only time will tell.

The recidivism data for the Federal Bureau of Prisons were even more problematic. The United States Sentencing Commission has tracked recidivism post implementation of the federal sentencing guidelines. The most recent report (2017) examines 25,431 offenders who were released into the community (either from federal prison or on to probation) in calendar year 2005. The federal data indicated that as criminal history score increased, the recidivism rate increased sharply. While the recidivism rate for category one offenders was a respectable 33.8 percent, the offenders with serious prior records of crime reflected a very high probability of recidivating, reaching a high of 80 percent for category 6. Clearly, federal sentencing reform and the de-emphasis of rehabilitation is correlated with these alarming recidivism data. Federal sentencing guidelines may or may not have eliminated discretion and disparity, while at the same time increasing fairness, equity, and transparency, but said guidelines surely did not have positive effects on recidivism.

Chapter Nine thus established that the present issue with respect to prisoner reentry has been influenced by external macro level factors like the baby boom and its effects on crime rates. But it has also been adversely affected by the advent of determinate sentencing models which have abandoned rehabilitation, have abolished parole, and have thereby exacerbated the smooth and successful reentry of inmates back into society.

In Chapter 10 we reviewed a National Reentry Resource Center's 2017 progress report on prisoner reentry which indicated five areas where progress had been made in the ways in which state and local government approaches to reentry and recidivism reduction are fundamentally different today than they were fifteen years ago. These areas were (1) state and local priority to reduce recidivism; (2) constituencies outside criminal justice; (3) scientific advances; (4) recidivism tracking; and (5) promising results.

We also reviewed the National Reentry Resource Center's position on six functional areas where further progress needs to be accomplished: (1) align state and local policy with what research demonstrates is effective in reducing recidivism: (2) develop a workforce that understands, embraces, and applies the latest research; (3) improve state and local governments' capacity to collect and analyze data; (4) monitor and assure quality of programs and services: (5) increase investment in effective programs, services, and supervision; and (6) develop additional knowledge.

Our position on these priorities is that they are certainly the optimal issues that must be addressed. However, it has been nineteen years since Petersilia and Travis raised the topic of prisoner reentry and surely one might expect that most, if not all, these issues would already be a long way towards optimum fulfillment. Unfortunately, such is not the case.

Chapter 10 also addressed the main goal of this book–to provide an evidenced-based model which addresses the incarceration of offenders with co-occurring disorders, and then the implementation of intervention strategies which track towards the transition of these offenders from the institutional setting back into the community. We noted that we searched far and wide for such a model. Our search did not produce a workable model that could be applied to both prisons and jails as opposed to just jails, and which detailed both the institutional setting as well as the community reentry setting until we came across the Continuum of Care™ model of The GEO Group, Inc. The GEO Continuum of Care is a trademarked approach for enhanced in-custody offender rehabilitation programming, including cognitive behavioral treatment, which is then integrated with post–release support services. The GEO continuum of care utilizes enhanced versions of five components: (1); Assessment; (2) Counseling; (3) Intervention; (4) Transition; and (5) Aftercare.

We reported that The Geo Group has had more than 30,000 daily participants in evidence-based programming worldwide. In the past ten years, GEO has awarded more than 10,000 GEDs through the company's in-prison academic programs. Over the last decade, approximately 60,000 inmates have achieved completion certificates from a variety of GEO vocational programs. Through GEO's treatment services, over 100,000 inmates have completed substance abuse and therapeutic programs in the last decade. Thus, the GEO continuum of care model has been extensively tested. We believed that the GEO Group's model fulfills all the requirements that our results indicated are necessary for offenders who have co-occurring disorders.

Based on the four major findings of this research evaluation, we provided below an outline of the components necessary to identify, treat, and release offenders with co-occurring disorders back into society. During the incarceration period, we see three major components.

First, screening for substance abuse and mental health disorders should take place with every inmate during the intake process. Mandatory screening will ensure that inmates are placed in appropriate settings within the institution but may also establish the need for clinical assessment to diagnose more specifically and clearly the presence of co-occurring disorders. Screening is easily implemented by correctional facilities, as most instruments do not require trained or licensed clinicians to conduct the instruments (see Chapter 3: Figures 3-1, 3-2, 3-3).

Second, however, our preference is that all inmates should be assessed at intake. Early assessment would provide faster access to support and resources inside the facility. It would also allow correctional staff to develop a plan tailored to the individual before any time is lost with unnecessary or incorrect programming. This is crucial in county jails where inmates generally serve up to two or two and a half years of prison time. Also, many inmates are unwilling to participate in multiple interviews or tests, thus reducing the number of sessions to just the assessment would ensure a better rapport but could also increase the likelihood of truthful answers. Further, screening instruments may lead to false negatives, where individuals who are suffering from either mental health or substance use disorders may be missed and not receive an assessment that would later inform correctional agents of the individuals' true diagnosis. Skipping directly to the assessment would eliminate the possibility of delayed assessment or no assessment at all. We have identified the assessment instruments in Chapter 3: Figures 3-4, 3-5, 3-6.

Third, treatment for the co-occurring disorders is the major component during the incarceration stage. We have borrowed the approach of the GEO Group because it seems comprehensive and targets the specific disorders with focused interventions. Naturally, clinicians are free to choose their own therapeutic interventions. As noted, it is crucial for the treatment of co-occurring disorders to commence as quickly as possible in county jails and it is likely that treatment will necessarily have to continue after release. We have also identified the need for academic and vocational programs to reduce the recidivism risk of these factors.

The second major component in our model is reentry planning. In this research we found that reentry/discharge planning suffered from two defects. First, the planning occurred too close to the time of release to be effective. There was just not sufficient time to coordinate the community resources that would be required to address the risks and needs of the offenders. Second, we also found that the services identified were too generic and did not appear to be calibrated to the risks that were identified by the LS/CMI. Both of these defects need to be eliminated if offender reentry has any chance at all of being successful.

Thus, in our model, reentry planning involves the following activities.

First, the risks and needs of each specific offender must be scored via the LS/CMI or a comparable instrument. The LS/CMI includes eight major subscales which cover important risks and the identification of crucial everyday services and needs.

Second, after risk and needs assessment is accomplished, reentry planning should formalize a treatment plan for the individual offender. Most important, reentry planning should identify and make arrangements with community-based agencies who will provide the specific treatments and services.

The third major component of our proposed model is post-release support. We envision this as a heavy case management function to assure that reentry is occurring in accord with the discharge plan and the offender is embracing the plan. Thus, case management must ensure continual communication with the offender personally and with his family and work location. The major activity of the case management is to conduct continual monitoring of the offender after release. Is he receiving the required treatment as identified by his risk scores? Is he receiving the required services as identified by his needs assessment? Strong case management upon release into the community and the continual monitoring of the offender will ensure the greatest chances for successful reentry.

We believe that the present study has provided important empirical results validating that the above model should be implemented and evaluated to determine if it qualifies as a best practice approach to the incarceration of offenders with co-occurring disorders, and then, the reentry of these offenders back into society.

References

Abram K.M., and Teplin L.A. (1991). "Co-occurring disorders among mentally ill jail detainees: Implications for public policy." *American Psychologist*, 46, 1036-1045.

Abram, K.M., Teplin, L.A., and McClelland, G.M. (2003). "Comorbidity of severe psychiatric disorders and substance use disorders among women in jail." *American Journal of Psychiatry*, 160, 1007-1010.

Abrantes A, Hoffmann N.G., and Anton R (2005). "Prevalence of co-occurring disorders among juveniles committed to detention centers." *International Journal of Offender Therapy and Comparative Criminology*, 49, 79-193.

Afshartous, D. and Preston, R.A. (2011). "Key results of interaction models with centering." *Journal of Statistics Education*, 19, 1-24.

Aiken, L.S., and West, S.G. (1991). *Multiple Regression: Testing and interpreting interactions*. Thousand Oaks: Sage.

AllGov.com California Department of Corrections and Rehabilitation. http://www.allgov.com/usa/ca/departments/independent-agencies/department_of_corrections_and_rehabilitation?agencyid=223

Allison, P.D. (1977). "Testing for interaction in multiple regression." *American Journal of Sociology*, 83, 144-153.

—. (1999). *Multiple regression: A primer*. Thousand Oaks, CA: Pine Forge Press.

American Psychiatric Association. (1994). *Diagnostic and Statistical Manual of Mental Disorders (DSM-IV)*. (4th ed.). Washington, DC.

Baillargeon, J., Binswanger, I.A., Penn, J.V., Williams, B.A., and Murray, O.J., (2009a). "Psychiatric disorders and repeat incarcerations; the revolving door." *American Journal of Psychiatry*, 166, 103-109.

Baillargeon, J., Williams, B.A., Mellow, J., Harzke, A.J., Hoge, S.K., Baillargeon, G., and Greifinger, R.B. (2009b). "Parole revocation among prison inmates with psychiatric and substance use disorders." *Psychiatric Services*, 60, 1516-1521.

Ballotpedia.org (1994). https://ballotpedia.org/California_Proposition_184,_Three_Strikes_Sentencing_Initiative_(1994).

Balyakina, E., Mann, C., Ellison, M., Sivernell, R., Fulda, K.G., Sarai, S.K, and Cardarelli, R. (2013). "Risk of future offense among probationers with co-occurring substance use and mental health disorders." *Community Mental Health Journal*, 50, 288-295.

Baron, R.M., and Kenny, D.A. (1986). "The moderator-mediator variable distinction in social psychological research: Conceptual, strategic and statistical considerations." *Journal of Personality and Social Psychology*, 51, 1173-1182

Beck, A.J. (2006). "The importance of successful reentry to jail population growth." Presented at the Urban Institute's Jail Reentry Roundtable, June 27, 2006. www.urban.org/projects/reentry-roundtable/upload/beck.PPT.

Begun, A.L., Early, T.J. and Hodge, A. (2016). "Mental health and substance abuse service engagement by men and women during community reentry following incarceration." *Administration Policy and Mental Health*, 43, 207-218.

Blandford, A.M. and Osher, F.C. (2013). "Guidelines for the successful transition of individuals with behavioral health disorders from jail and prison." Delmar, NY: SAMHSA's GAINS Center for Behavioral Health and Justice Transformation.

Blumstein, A., Cohen, J., Roth, J. A., and Visher, C. A. (Eds.). (1986). Criminal careers and career criminals, vol. I, II. Washington, DC: National Academy Press.

Braude, L. and Miller, N. (2011). "RSAT training tool: Understanding co-occurring disorders and applying integrated treatment strategies for adult correctional populations." Sudbury, MA: Advocates for Human Potential, Inc.

Brockway, Z.R. (1870). "The ideal of a true prison system for a state." Paper Presented to the National Congress on Penitentiary and Reformatory Discipline, Cincinnati, Ohio, October 12, 1870.

Bronson, J., Stroop, J., Zimmer, S., and Berzofsky, M. (2017). "Drug use, dependence, and abuse among state prisoners and jail inmates, 2007-2009." Washington, DC: U.S. Bureau of Justice Statistics.

Brown, J. D. (1996). *Testing in language programs*. Upper Saddle River, NJ: Prentice Hall Regents.

California Department of Corrections and Rehabilitation (2018). "2017 outcome evaluation report: An examination of offenders released in fiscal year 2012-13." Office of Research, June, 2018

Cameron, A.C. and Trivedi, P.K. (1998). *Regression analysis of count data*. Cambridge University Press.

Cameron IM, Cunningham L, Crawford JR, Eagles JM, Eisen SV, Lawton K, Naji S, Hamilton RJ. (2007). "Psychometric properties of the BASIS-24© (Behaviour and Symptom Identification Scale-Revised) mental health outcome measure." *International Journal of Psychiatry in Clinical Practice*, 11:36-43.

Campbell, Donald T. and Julian C. Stanley, *Experimental and quasi-experimental designs for research*. Rand McNally and Company, 1966.

Carson, E. A. and Sobel, W.J. (2012). "Prisoners in 2011," BJS Bulletin, December 2012, NCJ 239808.

Carroll, J.F.X. and McGinley, J.J. (2000). Mental Health Screening Form-III https://idph.iowa.gov/Portals/1/Files/SubstanceAbuse/jackson_mentalhealth_screeningtool.pdf

Chandler, R., Peters, R., Field, G., and Juliano-Bult, D. (2004). "Challenges in implementing evidence-based treatment practices for co-occurring disorders in the criminal justice system." *Behavioral Sciences and the Law*, 22, 431-448.

Chiles, J. A., Cleve, E. V., Jemelka, R. P., and Trupin, E. W. (1990). "Substance abuse and psychiatric disorders in prison inmates." *Hospital and Community Psychiatry*, 41, 1132-1134.

Center for Prisoner Health and Human Rights. (2016). http://www.prisonerhealth.org/educational-resources/factsheets-2/incarceration-substance-abuse-and-addiction/

Cohen, L.E., and K.C. Land (1987) "Age structure and crime: Symmetry versus asymmetry and the projection of crime rates through the 1990s." *American Sociological Review* 52 (170-183).

Cook, T.D. and Campbell, D.T. (1979) *Quasi-experimentation: Design and analysis issues for field settings*. Boston: Houghton Mifflin Company.

Council of State Governments Justice Center. (2017). "Reducing recidivism: States deliver results."

Dennis, M.L., White, M., Titus, J.C., and Unsicker, J. (2008). "Global appraisal of needs: Administration guide for the GAIN and related measures, Version 5." Normal, IL: Chestnut Health Systems. Retrieved from https://chestnut.app.box.com/v/GAIN-I-Materials/file/63671257181

Derogatis, L.R. (1993). "BSI brief symptom inventory: Administration, scoring, and procedure manual." (4th Ed.). Minneapolis, MN: National Computer Systems.

Ditton, P. (1999). "Mental health and treatment of inmates and probationers." Washington, D.C.: U.S. Department of Justice, Office of Justice Programs, Bureau of Justice Statistics.

Ditton, P.M. and Wilson, D.J. (1999). "Truth in sentencing in state prisons, special report." Washington, DC: U.S. Department of Justice, Bureau of Justice Statistics, NCJ 170032.

Drayton, M. (2009). "The Minnesota multiphasic personality inventory-2 (MMPI-2)." Occupational Medicine, 59(2), 135-136. https://doi.org/10.1093/occmed/kqn182

Durose, M.R., Cooper, A.D., and Snyder, H.N. (2014). "Recidivism of prisoners released in 30 states in 2005: Patterns from 2005 to 2010," U.S. Department of Justice, Office of Justice Programs, Bureau of Justice Statistics. http://www.bjs.gov/index.cfm?ty=pbdetail&iid=4986 (accessed September 29, 2015).

Elmira Prison http://www.correctionhistory.org/html/chronicl/docs2day/elmira.html

Eisen, S., Gerena, M., Ranganathan, G., Esch, D., and Idiculla, T. (2006). "Reliability and validity of the BASIS-24 mental health survey for Whites, African Americans, and Latinos." *Journal of Behavioral Health Services and Research*, 33(3), 304-323.

Edens, J. F., and Ruiz, M. A. (2006). "On the validity of validity scales: The importance of defensive responding in the prediction of institutional misconduct." *Psychological Assessment*, 18, 220-224.

Feldstein, S., and Miller, W. (2007). "Does subtle screening for substance abuse work? A review of the substance abuse subtle screening inventory (SASSI)." *Addiction*, 102, 41-50.

Fellner, J., and Maurer, M. (1998). "Losing the right to vote: The impact of felony disenfranchisement laws in the United States." The Sentencing Project, Washington, DC.

First, M. B., Spitzer, R. L., Gibbon, M., and Williams, J. B. (2001). *Users guide for the structured clinical interview for DSM-IV-TR Axis I Disorders - Research version*. New York, NY: Biometrics Research Department.

Framingham, J. (2016). Millon Clinical Multiaxial Inventory (MCMI-III). Psych Central. Retrieved on July 9, 2018, from https://psychcentral.com/lib/millon-clinical-multiaxial-inventory-mcmi-iii/

Gallagher, S.M., Penn, P.E., Brooks, A.J., and Feldman, J. (2006). "Comparing the CAAPE, A New Assessment Tool for Co-occurring Disorders, with the SCID." *Psychiatric Rehabilitation Journal*, 30, 63-65,

GEO Group. Inc. (2018). *GEO continuum of care™ 2017 annual report.*

Glaser, D. (1964). *The effectiveness of a prison and parole system.* New York: Bobbs-Merrill.

Guerino, P.M., P.M. Harrison, and W. Sabol. (2011). "Prisoners in 2010." NCJ 236096. Washington, D.C.: U.S. Department of Justice, Bureau of Justice Statistics, http://www.bjs.gov/content/pub/pdf/p10.pdf.

Greenberg, D. (1985). "Age, crime and social explanation." *American Journal of Sociology* 91: 1-21.

Grisso, T. (2006) "Jail screening assessment tool (JSAT): Guidelines for screening in jails." *Psychiatric Services*, 57(7).

Hasin, D., Samet, S., Nunes, E., Meydan, J., Matseoane, K., and Waxman, R. (2006). "Diagnosis of co-morbid psychiatric disorders in substance users assessed with the psychiatric research interview for substance and mental disorders for DSM-IV." *American Journal of Psychiatry*, 163(4), 689-696.

Hatch, O.G. (1993). "The role of Congress in sentencing: The United States sentencing commission, mandatory minimum sentences, and the search for a certain and effective sentencing system." 28 L. REV. 185, 186, Wake Forest.

Hirsch, A.J. (1992). *The Rise of the Penitentiary: Prisons and Punishment in Early America.* New Haven, CT: Yale University Press.

Hofer, P., Loeffler, C., Blackwell, K., and Valentino, P. (2004). *Fifteen years of guidelines sentencing: An assessment of how well the federal criminal justice system is achieving the goals of sentencing reform.* United States Sentencing Commission.

Hoffmann, N.G. (2000). *CAAPE (Comprehensive Addictions and Psychological Evaluation) Manual*. Smithfield, R.I.: Evince Clinical Assessments.

Houck, K. D., and Loper, A. B. (2002). "The relationship of parenting stress to adjustment among mothers in prison." *American Journal of Orthopsychiatry*, 72(4), 548-558.

Houser, K. and Belenko, S. (2015). "Disciplinary responses to misconduct among female prison inmates with mental illness, substance use disorders, and co-occurring disorders." *Psychiatric Rehabilitation Journal*, 38, 24-34. http://psycnet.apa.org/doi/10.1037/prj0000110

Howell, R. (2004). "Sentencing reform lessons: From the sentencing reform act of 1984 to the Feeney Amendment." *Journal of Criminal Law and Criminology*, 94, 1069-1103.

H.R. 1593 "The second chance act of 2007: Community safety through recidivism prevention," 110th Congress 2008 (also known as Pub. L. 110-199).

Hughes, T. and D.J. Wilson. (2002). *Reentry trends in the United States*. Washington, D.C.: U.S. Department of Justice, Bureau of Justice Assistance, 2002. bjs.ojp.usdoj.gov/content/pub/pdf/reentry.pdf

Hunt, E., Peters, R.H., and Kremling, J. (2015). "Behavioral health treatment history among persons in the justice system: Findings from the arrestee drug abuse monitoring II program." *Psychiatric Rehabilitation Journal*, 38, 7-15. http://dx.doi.org/10.1037/prj0000132

Inside CDCR (2015) "A decade ago, a new name affirmed mission of CDCR." California Department of Correction and Rehabilitation.

Institute of Behavioral Research. (2007). *Texas Christian University Drug Screen II.* Fort Worth: Texas Christian University, Institute of Behavioral Research. Available at ibr.tcu.edu

James, D.J. and Glaze, L.E. (2006). "Mental health problems of prison and jail inmates." Washington, D.C.: U.S. Department of Justice, Office of Justice Programs, Bureau of Justice Statistics.

Jones, G.Y. and Hoffman, N.G. (2006). "Alcohol dependence: international policy implications for prison populations." *Substance Abuse Treatment, Prevention, and Policy*, 1, 33-38.

Johnston, N. (2000). *Forms of constraint: A history of prison architecture*. Urbana. IL: University of Illinois Press.

Johnson, P.E. (1978). "California's determinate sentencing statute: History and issues." University of California Berkeley, Law Scholarship Repository, *1 Determinate Sentencing: Reform or Regression*, 13-58.

Karberg, J.C. and James, D.J. (2005). "Substance dependence, abuse, and treatment of jail inmates, 2002." NCJ 209588. Washington, D.C.: U.S. Department of Justice, Bureau of Justice Statistics. bjs.ojp.usdoj.gov/content/pub/pdf/sdatji02.pdf.

Kassebaum, G., Ward, D., and Wilnet, D.P. (1971). *Prison treatment and parole survival: An Empirical Assessment.* New York: Wiley.

Lamb, H. R., Weinberger, L. E., and Gross, B. H. (2004). "Mentally ill persons in the criminal justice system: Some perspectives." *Psychiatric Quarterly*, 75, 107-126.

La Vigne, N.G. and Kachnowski, V. (2003). *A portrait of prisoner reentry in Maryland.* Washington, DC: The Urban Institute.

Langan, P.A. and Levin, D. (2002). *Recidivism of prisoners released in 1994, Bureau of Justice Statistics special report* NCJ 193427. Washington, DC: U.S. Department of Justice, 2002.

Lazowski, L.E. (2016). "Estimates of the reliability and criterion validity of the adult SASSI-4." Springville, IN: The SASSI Institute.

Lipton, D.S., Martinson, R., and Wilks, J. (1975). *The effectiveness of correctional treatment: A survey of treatment evaluation studies.* Westport, CT: Praeger Publishers.

Luttrell, M.H. (1991). "The impact of the sentencing reform act on prison management." *Federal Probation*, 55, 54-57.

Mandell, W. (1967). "Surgical and social rehabilitation of adult offenders: Final report." Montefiore Hospital and Medical Center, With Staten Island Mental Health Society. New York City Department of Correction.

Martinson, R. (1974). "What works? Questions and answers about prison reform." *The Public Interest*, 35, 22-54.

Megargee, E. I., and Carbonell, J. L. (1995). "Use of the MMPI-2 in correctional settings." In Y. S. Ben-Porath, J. R. Graham, G. C. N. Hall, R. Hirschman, and M. Zaragoza (Eds.), *Forensic applications of the MMPI-2.* 127-159. Thousand Oaks, CA: Sage Publications.

Messick, S. (1989). "Validity." In R.L. Linn (Ed.), *Educational measurement* (3rd ed.). 13-103. New York: Macmillan.

Miller, G.A. (1985). The substance abuse subtle screening inventory (SASSI) manual. (2nd ed.). Springville, IN: The SASSI Institute. *Mistretta v. United States*, 488 U.S. 361 (1989).

Mohamed MN, Marican S, Othman MH, Thurairajasingam, S. and Ali, N. (2017). Validation of addiction severity index 5th edition, Bahasa Melayu version (asi-5-bm). MOJ Addiction Medicine Therapy 2017;4(2):243–247. DOI: 10.15406/mojamt.2017.04.00075

Mumola, C.J. (2000). *Incarcerated parents and their children.* Bureau of Justice Statistics: Special Report NCJ 182335. Washington, DC: U.S. Department of Justice.

Mumola, C.J. and J.C. Karberg, J.C. (2006). *Drug Use and dependence, state and federal prisoners, 2004.* NCJ 213530. Washington, D.C.: U.S. Department of Justice, Bureau of Justice Statistics. bjs.ojp.usdoj.gov/content/pub/pdf/dudsfp04.pdf.

Murphy, J.G. (1970). *Kant: The Philosophy of Right.* London: Macmillan.

Nagel, I. (1990). "Structuring sentencing discretion: The new federal sentencing guidelines." *Journal of Criminal Law and Criminology*, 80, 883-943.

National Center on Addiction and Substance Abuse. (2010). “Behind bars II: Substance abuse and America’s prison population.” New York: Columbia University.

National Center on Addiction and Substance Abuse. (1998). “Behind bars: Substance abuse and America's prison population.” New York: Columbia University.

National Council on Crime and Delinquency (1972). Model Sentencing Act.

National Institutes of Health. (2010). *Fact Sheet: Addiction in the criminal justice system*. Washington, DC.

National Public Radio (2009). “The evolution of California's three strikes law.” October 2009.

National Reentry Resource Center. (2017). *Making people’s transition from prison and jail to the community safe and successful: A snapshot of national progress in reentry.* Bureau of Justice Assistance.

Negrete. J., Collins, J., Turner, N., and Skinner, W. (2004). “The centre for addiction and mental health concurrent disorders screener.” Canadian Journal Of Psychiatry, 49(12), 843-850. https://doi.org/10.1177/070674370404901208

Nicholls, T.L., Roesch, R., Olley, M.C., Ogloff, J.R.P., and Hemphill, J.F. (2005). *Jail screening assessment tool (JSAT): Guidelines for mental health screening in jails.* Burnaby, BC: Simon Fraser University, Mental Health, Law, and Policy Institute.

Norton, E.C. and Ai. C. (2004). “Computing interaction effects and standard errors in logit and probit models.” *Stata Journal*, 4,103-116.

Osher, F. (2013). *Integrating mental health and substance abuse services for justice-involved persons with co-occurring disorders*. Substance Abuse and Mental Health Services Administration. Gains Center.

Osher, F., Steadman, H.J., and Barr, H. (2003). “A best practice approach to community reentry from jails for inmates with co-occurring disorders: The APIC model.” *Crime and Delinquency*, 49, 79-96.

Perkey, H., Sinclair, S., Blais, M., Stein, M., Neal, P., Pierson, A., and Slavin-Mulford, J. (2018). “External validity of the psychiatric diagnostic screening questionnaire (PDSQ) in a clinical sample.” *Psychiatry Research*, 261, 14-20.

Peters, R.H., Wexler, H.K. and Lurigio, A.J. (2015). “Co-occurring substance use and mental disorders in the criminal justice system: A new frontier of clinical practice and research.” *Psychiatric Rehabilitation Journal*, 38, 1–6.

Peters, R.H., Bartoi, M.G., and Sherman, P.B. (2008). "Screening and assessment of co-occurring disorders in the justice system." Delmar, NY: CMHS National GAINS Center.

Peters, R. H., LeVasseur, M. E., and Chandler, R. K. (2004). "Correctional treatment for co-occurring disorders: Results of a national survey." *Behavioral Sciences and the Law*, 22(4), 563-584.

Peters, R. (2018). "Best practices in screening and assessment for people with co-occurring substance use and mental health disorders in the criminal justice system: Review of available instruments and how to select a tool that works for your reentry program." Retrieved from: https://csgjusticecenter.org/nrrc/webinars/screening-and-assessment-best-practices-for-people-with-co-occurring-substance-use-and-mental-disorders-cods/

Petersilia, J. (2001). "Prisoner reentry: Public safety and reintegration challenges." *The Prison Journal*, 81, 360-375.

Petersilia, J. (1999). "Parole and prisoner reentry in the United States." In M. Tonry and J. Petersilia (Eds.), *Prisons,* 479-529. Chicago: University of Chicago Press.

Pettersson, A., Modin, S., Wahlstrom, R., Hammarberg, S., and Krakau, I. (2018). "The mini-international neuropsychiatric interview is useful and well accepted as part of the clinical assessment for depression and anxiety in primary care: A mixed methods study." *BMC Family Practice*, 19(1). https://doi.org/10.1186/s12875-017-0674-5

Policy Research Institute (2005). *Brief jail mental health screening*.

Reno, J. (2000, February). "Remarks of the Honorable Janet Reno on reentry court initiative." Presented at John Jay College of Criminal Justice, New York. https://www.justice.gov/archive/ag/speeches/2000/doc2.htm

Retzlaff, P., Stoner, J., and Kleinsasser, D. (2002). "The use of the MCMI-III in the screening and triage of offenders." *International Journal of Offender Therapy and Comparative Criminology*, 46(3), 319-332.

Robison, J., and Smith, G. (1971). "The effectiveness of correctional programs." *Crime and Delinquency*, 17, 67-80.

Robison, J. Kevotkian, M. (1967), *Intensive treatment project: Phase II. Parole outcome: Interim report*. Research Report No. 27. California Department of Corrections, Youth and Adult Correctional Agency.

Royse, D., and Drude, K. (2008). "Screening drug abuse clients with the brief symptom inventory." *International Journal of the Addictions*, 847-857.

Ruiz, M.A., Peters, R., Sanchez, G., and Bates, J. (2009). "Psychometric properties of the mental health screening form III within a metropolitan jail." *Criminal Justice and Behavior*, 36(6), 607-619.

Sacks, S., Melnick, G., Coen, C., Banks, S., Friedmann, P., Grella, C., Knight, K. and Zlotnick, C. (2007). "CJDATS Co-occurring disorders screening instrument for mental disorders: A validation study." *Criminal Justice and Behavior: An International Journal*, 34(9), 1198-1215.

Sagi, P.C., and C.F. Wellford (1968). "Age composition and patterns of change in criminal statistics." *The Journal of Criminal Law, Criminology and Police Science* 59(1): 29-36.

Scott, C.K., Dennis, M.L., and Lurigio, A.J. (2015). "Comorbidity among female detainees in drug treatment: An exploration of internalizing and externalizing disorders." *Psychiatric Rehabilitation Journal*, 38, 35-44. http://psycnet.apa.org/doi/10.1037/prj0000134

Sheehan, D. V., Lecrubier, Y., Sheehan, K. H., Amorim, P., Janavs. J., Weiller, E. (1998). "The MINI-international neuropsychiatric interview (MINI): The development and validation of a structured diagnostic psychiatric interview for DSM-IV and ICD-10." *Journal of Clinical Psychiatry*, 20, 22-33.

Skinner, HA, (1982). "The drug abuse screening test." *Addictive Behavior*, 7(4):363-371.

Staton-Tindall, M., Harp, K.L.H., Minieri, A, Oser, C.,Webster, J.M., Havens, J., and Leukefeld, C. (2015). An exploratory study of mental health and HIV risk behavior among drug-using rural women in jail. *Psychiatric Rehabilitation Journal*, 38, 45-54.

Steadman, H., Fabisiak, S., Dvoskin, S., Edward Holohean, E. (1989). "A Survey of Mental Disability among State Prison Inmates." *Hospital and Community Psychiatry*, 38, 1086-1090.

Steadman, H., Scott, J., Osher, F., Agnese, T., and Robbins, P. (2005). "Validation of the brief jail mental health screen." *Psychiatric Services*, 56 (7), 816-822.

Steadman, H.J., Osher, F. C., Robbins, P. C., Case, B., and Samuels, S. (2009). "Prevalence of serious mental illness among jail inmates," *Psychiatric Services*, 60, 761-765.

Steffensmeier, D., and Harer, M.D. (1987). "Is the crime rate really falling?" *Journal of Research in Crime and Delinquency*, 24, 23-48.

St. John, P. (2014). "Gov. Jerry Brown's prison reforms haven't lived up to his billing." *Los Angeles Times*, Jun 21, 2014.

Substance Abuse and Mental Health Services Administration. (2015). "Screening and assessment of co-occurring disorders in the justice system." HHS Publication No. (SMA)-15-4930. Rockville, MD: Substance Abuse and Mental Health Services Administration.

Substance Abuse and Mental Health Services Administration. (2011). *The TEDS report: Characteristics of probation and parole admissions aged 18 or older*. Rockville, MD.: Center for Behavioral Health Statistics and Quality.

The Second Chance Act of 2007 https://apa.org/about/gr/science/advocacy/2008/second-chance-act-2007.pdf_*The Sentencing Reform Act*. (1984). Pub. L. No. 98-473, § 236,98 Stat. 1837,2033 (1984).

Teplin, L. A. (1990). "Detecting disorder: The treatment of mental illness among jail detainees." *Journal of Consulting and Clinical Psychology*, 58, 233-236.

—. (1994). "Psychiatric and substance abuse disorders among male urban detainees." *American Journal of Public Health*, 84, 290-293.

Teplin, L. A., Abram, K. M., and McClelland, G. M. (1996). "Prevalence of psychiatric disorders among incarcerated women: Pretrial jail detainees." *Archives of General Psychiatry*, 53, 505-512.

Titus, J.C., Dennis, M.L., Lennox, R., and Scott, C.K. (2008). "Development and validity of the internal mental distress and behavioral complexity scales in the global appraisal of individual needs (GAIN)." *Journal of Behavioral Health Services and Research*, 35:2.

Titus, J. C., Feeney, T., Smith, D. C., Rivers, T. L., Kelly, L. L., and Dennis, M. D. (2013). *GAIN-Q3 3.2: Administration, clinical interpretation, and brief intervention*. Normal, IL: Chestnut Health Systems.

Torrens, M., Serrano, D., Astals, M., Perez-Dominguez, G., and Martin-Santos, R. (2004). "Diagnosing comorbid psychiatric disorders in substance abusers: Validity of the Spanish version of psychiatric research interview for substance and mental disorders and the structured clinical." *American Journal of Psychiatry*, 161(7), 1231-37.

Tracy, P.E. and Carkin, D.M. (2017). "Testing the criterion validity of the CAAPE for screening co-occurring disorders among jail inmates." *Journal of Psychology and Behavioral Science*, 4, 59-69

Tracy, P.E., Wolfgang, M.E., and Figlio, R.M. (1990) *Delinquency careers in two birth cohorts*. New York: Plenum Press.

United States Sentencing Commission (1991). *The federal sentencing guidelines: A report on the operation of the guidelines system and short-term impacts on disparity in sentencing, use of incarceration, and prosecutorial discretion and plea bargaining.*

Urban Institute (2006). "Understanding the challenges of prisoner reentry: Research findings from the Urban Institute's prisoner reentry portfolio."

Visher, C. A. (1986) "The rand inmate surveys: A reanalysis". In A. Blumstein, J. Cohen, J. A. Roth, and C. A. Visher, (Eds.), *Criminal careers and career criminals*, vol. II (pp. 161-211). Washington, DC: National Academy Press.

Vitiello, M. (1997). "Three strikes: Can we return to rationality." *Journal of Criminal Law and Criminology*, 87, 395-481.

Von Hirsch, A. (1976). *Doing justice: The choice of punishments*. Boston, MA: Northeastern University Press.

Von Hirsch, A. (1987). *Past or future crimes: Deservedness and dangerousness in the sentencing of criminals*. New Brunswick, NJ: Rutgers University Press. Walnut Street Prison. http://law.jrank.org/pages/11192/Walnut-Street-Prison.html

Walters, G.D. (2007). "Using Poisson class regression to analyze count data in correctional and forensic psychology." *Criminal Justice and Behavior*, 34: 1659-1674.

Wang, E., Rogers, R., Giles, C., Diamond, P., Herrington-Wang, L., and Taylor, E.R. (1998). "A pilot study of the personality assessment inventory (PAI) in corrections: assessment of malingering, suicide risk, and aggression in male inmates." *Behavioral Sciences and the Law*, 15(4), 469-482.

Wellford, C. (1973). "Age composition and the increase in recorded crime." *Criminology* 11(1): 61-70.

Wolfgang, M.E., Figlio, R.M. and Sellin, T. (1972) *Delinquency in a birth cohort*. Chicago: University of Chicago Press.

Wolfgang, M.E., Thornberry, T.P. and Figlio, R.M. (1987) *From boy to man, from delinquency to crime*. Chicago: University of Chicago Press.

Zabora, J., Brintzenhofeszoc K., Jacobsen, P., Curbow, B., Piantadosi, S., Hooker, C., (2001). "A new psychological screening instrument for use with cancer patients." Psychosomatics, 42(3), 241-246.

Zimmerman, M. and Mattia, J., (2001). "The psychiatric diagnostic screening questionnaire: Development, reliability, and validity." *Comprehensive Psychiatry*, 42, 175-189.

Zimmerman, M. (2002). *The psychiatric diagnostic screening questionnaire manual*. Western Psychological Services.